# History of the Cumberland Presbyterian Church in Texas

## By Thomas H. Campbell

March 2017

Memphis, Tennessee

Historical Foundation of the
Cumberland Presbyterian Church
and the Cumberland Presbyterian Church in America

The primary portion of this book was originally published by the Cumberland Presbyterian Publishing House in 1936. The period in which the original manuscript was prepared should be kept in mind when reading this volume. No changes have been made to the original text. Funded, in part, by your contributions to Our United Outreach.

The 1936 editorial committee were Rev. Thomas H. Campbell, Mrs. H. R. Allen, and Miss Helen Bradford.

First printing in this format, March 2017.

ISBN-13: 978-1945929090
ISBN-10: 194592909X

OUR UNITED OUTREACH
Made Possible In Part By Your Tithe To Our United Outreach

This Volume Is Dedicated to

# THE CUMBERLAND PRESBYTERAN YOUTH
## OF TEXAS

That by this record of how our church in
Texas has carried on for more than a
century and of how its men and
women, those who are still with
us and those who have gone
before, have been used of
God in the salvation of
souls, you may be in-
spired to a greater
life of service for
Christ and the
church

# FOREWORD

In response to a memorial from Dallas Presbytery, the Synod of Texas of the Cumberland Presbyterian Church in session at Olton, Texas, October, 1934, appointed a commission composed of Revs. M. F. Allen, Alba H. Bates, H. R. Allen, and Thomas H. Campbell, and Ruling Elder Bun E. Rodden, to whom was committed the work of preparing an historical program setting forth the activities of the Cumberland Presbyterian Church in the making of Texas history, same to be sponsored and presented by said commission in connection with the Texas Centennial Exposition to be held at Dallas in 1936.

Those who initiated the move resulting in the appointment of this commission had in mind particularly the arrangement and presentation of pageantry depicting the origin and achievements of the Cumberland Presbyterian Church in Texas, together with the assembling of materials for an historical exhibit. The commission in planning for these centennial celebrations felt that if the interest thus awakened was to be conserved to greatest advantage, the history of our church in Texas, from the time when Sumner Bacon heard and answered the call to preach the gospel in Texas until the present, should be published in book form. Accordingly, a committee was appointed, consisting of Mrs. H. R. Allen, Miss Helen Bradford, and the writer (who was made chairman of the committee), to have the oversight of the preparation of this historical volume. Plans for publishing the history were subsequently approved by the synod in its 1935 meeting.

The responsibility which accompanied the chairmanship of this committee was accepted, not without a certain amount of pleasure over the prospect of engaging in a work of this kind, notwithstanding the consciousness of limitations by reason of a lack of those years of experience which enable one more correctly to interpret and evaluate the movements of history. This is a subject in which I have always been profoundly interested, however, and many times have I delighted in hearing from the lips of the older men and women the earlier history of the Cumberland Presbyterian Church in various portions of Texas where it has been my privilege to labor. Although no definite effort had been made to keep a record of the things thus learned, the information obtained stayed with me in a general way. If I did not recall the details, at least I remembered where they might be obtained.

Very little had been done toward the accomplishment of this work, however, until I was called to a work for the church which necessitated my removal from the state of Texas, so the greater part of the research work devolved upon others. Especially would we mention the valuable service rendered by Rev. H. R. Allen, secretary of the commission, who has traveled many hundreds of miles in locating and gaining access to sources where many important points of history have been obtained. Mrs. Allen, also, has engaged faithfully in the task of compiling and making available to us in typewritten form the data thus obtained, and, as a member of the committee, has reviewed the manuscript and made valuable suggestions.

Contacts have been made with members of the families of the ministers who made up the original Texas Presbytery, namely, Mrs. D. B. Wolfe and Mrs. Betty T. Wright, of Dallas, granddaughters of Rev. Sumner

Bacon, who have made available to us important papers bearing on the life and work of this pioneer Cumberland Presbyterian preacher of Texas, as well as contributing of those unwritten bits of history which have been handed down by word of mouth; Rev. J. M. Smith, age eighty-eight years, son of Rev. Mitchell Smith, and Mr. T. E. Davis, a grandson, both of whom live at Miles, Texas; and Judge Royal R. Watkins, of Dallas, grandson of Rev. Richard O. Watkins, first Protestant minister ever ordained on Texas soil, who made available to us the diary and autobiography of his grandfather, which have proved to be most valuable as sources of information on the earlier periods of history, and to which we have had occasion to refer frequently.

Many historical sketches of local congregations and biographical sketches of ministers and elders, too numerous to list here, have come into our hands. We have also examined the minutes of the General Assembly as far back as 1849, minutes of Texas Synod from the consolidation of the four synods in 1888 until the present, some presbyterial records of earlier date, extensive files of The Cumberland Presbyterian and The Cumberland Presbyterian Banner, copies of the Texas Observer, and other periodicals. Histories of Texas, local and county histories, and documents on file in the archives of the Republic of Texas in the state capitol at Austin have also been examined. A manuscript contributed by Rev. J. W. Pearson on the history of Tehuacana contains much information on the early history of Trinity University. We have also had access to the history of the woman's missionary work in Texas Synod, recently compiled by Mrs. J. H. Johnson, of Hubbard.

We would also express our gratitude to all those who have aided us in this work whose heritage is Cumberland Presbyterian though they themselves now find shelter in another fold. Especially would we mention the assistance so kindly rendered by Rev. B. A. Hodges, D.D., of Trinity University, who made available to us the minutes of the first three meetings of Texas Presbytery. The personal correspondence of those of us who have been engaged in this work has included quite a number of former Cumberland Presbyterians who have readily contributed of their store of information touching on the history of the church in localities where they have labored.

In the arrangement of this work we have made our chapters to conform to those periods into which the history of the Cumberland Presbyterian Church in Texas seemed naturally to divide itself. Naturally we have given a more detailed account of the earliest period leading up to the organization of Texas Synod than has been possible to follow throughout. From that time on, it has been impossible to follow anything like a strict chronological arrangement, as the church spread over a large territory and things were happening at so many different places at the same time. So we have endeavored to follow the plan of tracing the origin and early history of the church in the different localities, showing how the different presbyteries grew out of these beginnings, then concluding with a brief resume of the subsequent progress of the church in that particular locality. We have followed this through with the various presbyteries, considering each one in the period in which the presbytery was organized.

Although we have extended this work much beyond what was originally contemplated, we have had to limit the size of this work by a selection of such material as would best serve to illustrate the contribution which our denomination has made to the religious life and history of Texas.   To include the history of every congregation or the biography of every minister who has contributed to the furtherance of the Cumberland faith in Texas would be an impossibility. Then, too, the material in hand has been much more detailed concerning some localities than has been the case with others.   What we have sought to do is to present, as far as we have gone, an accurate, readable account of the origin, progress, trials, and triumphs of a branch of the church which was among the first Protestant denominations on Texas soil.

We cannot live on the achievements of the past; we have our present situations to face; but we gain much of our inspiration from the past.   We are building upon the foundations which others have laid, and if we would carry forward successfully the work which they have begun, we must know something of how they built.   With the hope that all who read may be inspired to a deeper consecration to Christ and to the interests of his kingdom; that somehow the imperfections of this work imposed by many limitations, not least of which has been the hurried preparation which has been required, may be overruled so that you may get a greater vision of Christ and a greater longing to make known to others his "whosoever will" gospel, we send forth this book on its mission.

T. H. C.

Nashville, Tenn.,
June 2, 1936.

# Chapter I

## SUMNER BACON AND HIS CO-LABORERS
### (1826-1843)

ALL great movements which have influenced the trend of history have had their pioneer spirits. The record of every worth while achievement carries us back to men and women who saw visions and dreamed dreams, and who dared to venture all for the realization of that thing the passion for which possessed their souls. If this be true in the material world, certainly it is no less true in the achievement of those things which have to do with the religious and spiritual life of a people. Christianity has produced many such pioneer spirits. It is not surprising, then, that in setting out to record the struggles and triumphs of a branch of the church which took its place among the first in the work of evangelizing that great empire of the Southwest known as Texas, we begin with the story of an adventurer.

\* \* \*

Sumner Bacon, the pioneer Cumberland Presbyterian preacher of Texas, was born in the historic state of Massachusetts, in the county of Worcester, on January 22, 1790.\* Bacon's father had great ambitions for his son and educated him for the legal profession, but when young Sumner attained his majority, instead of pursuing the career which his father had chosen for him, he mounted his horse one day and rode away.

\*From vital records, Auburn, Mass., as quoted in a letter to John Bacon, son of Sumner Bacon, from P. C. Bacon. Other facts concerning Bacon's life are taken from the original draft of a letter written by John Bacon to Mr. J. C. Coit.

In 1817 he enlisted in the United States army as a private, and two and a half years later received his discharge in the vicinity of Fayetteville, Arkansas, where he remained for several years, working most of the time as a surveyor.

Bacon's leaving home evidently was not impelled by any religious motive, for at that time he was not a Christian. In fact, he was an avowed disbeliever. In 1825 a revival meeting was held at Fayetteville under the auspices of the Cumberland Presbyterian Church, and in this meeting Sumner Bacon professed faith in Christ. Immediately he was impressed with the fact that he was called to the ministry and that Texas was his field. Thus the adventuresome spirit of Sumner Bacon was transformed, and he was called to a life of greater adventure for Christ.

*     *     *

The Cumberland Presbyterian Church, under the ministry of which Bacon was converted and to which he now attached himself, had originated several years before in that great spiritual awakening known as the revival of 1800, particularly as that revival of religion touched the Presbyterian congregations on the frontier of middle Tennessee and Kentucky. Its existence as a separate denomination dates from February 4, 1810, when three Presbyterian ministers — Finis Ewing, Samuel King, and Samuel McAdow—met at the home of the latter in Dickson County, Tennessee, and constituted an independent presbytery.

The events which led up to the separation from the Presbyterian Church are clearly set forth in the Circular Letter sent out by this presbytery at the time of its organization. Briefly the two underlying causes which brought into existence the Cumberland Presbyterian Church were, first, the question of the validity of the licensure and ordination of certain ministers who had not attained to the letter of the educational standards prescribed by the Presbyterian Church, and, second, a reaction against the fatalistic implications of the doctrine of predestination as set forth in the Confession of Faith of the Presbyterian Church. In both cases the differences which led to the formation of the new church resulted directly from the intense interest in spiritual things which characterized the revival.

The first was brought about by the pressing need for more preachers, which led to the suggestion that certain men of good talents who felt disposed to exercise their gifts in public exhortation be encouraged to preach, in order that the great need for more preachers might be supplied. Some of these men were eventually licensed and ordained, for which their presbytery (Cumberland) was brought to task by the appointment of a synodical commission which proceeded not only to forbid all the ministers whom Cumberland Presbytery had ordained, both learned and unlearned, from preaching as Presbyterians, but also to dissolve Cumberland Presbytery.

Of the three who helped to form the new church, Ewing and King were among the number who had been ordained by Cumberland Presbytery under the head of exceptional cases. McAdow was himself a graduate and had been ordained before he came to this section of the country, but was a member of the presbytery which the commission had proceeded illegally to dissolve. This is not to imply that Ewing and

King were not educated men, for what was meant by unlearned men was not the lack of a good English education, but the fact that they had not attained to the prescribed course of study, especially the study of Greek and Hebrew. They were living on the frontier in a sparsely settled country where the facilities for higher education were not to be had. They had entered the ministry under the pressure of a call to minister to those who were destitute of the means of grace, and with the approval of brethren who felt that aptness to teach was of greater importance than the attainment of human standards of education.

As to the doctrinal question, it was a case of the old bottles not being able to contain the new wine. In the midst of a great awakening of religious interest, where it was manifest that the Spirit of God was working in the hearts of the people, where men and women were crying out for mercy over their lost condition, and others rejoicing over finding new life in Christ, it was virtually impossible to hold on to a creed which was permeated with the teaching that Christ died for only a certain portion of the human race known as the elect, who alone would be saved, and whose "number is so certain and definite that it cannot be either increased or diminished."* It is no wonder, then, that some men saw the inconsistency of such a creed with what God was actually doing in their midst. This, then, was the other charge which the synodical commission above referred to, brought against Cumberland Presbytery, namely, that they had licensed and ordained men who had only been required

---

*Westminster Confession of Faith, chap. III, section IV.

to adopt the Confession of Faith in so far as they believed it to agree with the Word of God.

The new presbytery required its candidates to receive and adopt the Confession of Faith and Discipline of the Presbyterian Church "except the idea of fatality, that seems to be taught under the mysterious doctrine of predestination." Those who could receive the Confession of Faith without making this exception were not required to make any. The General Synod, which was constituted in 1813, further clarified the position of the Cumberland Presbyterian Church by adopting the following brief statement of points wherein Cumberland Presbyterians differed from the Presbyterian Church:

"1. That there are no eternal reprobates.

"2. That Christ died not for a part only, but for all mankind.

"3. That all infants dying in infancy are saved through Christ and the sanctification of the Spirit.

"4. That the Spirit of God operates on the world, or as co-extensively as Christ has made atonement, in such a manner as to leave all men inexcusable."

Such was the basis upon which the early Cumberland Presbyterian preachers went forth, following the tide of migration westward and preaching the gospel to the new settlements on the frontier. The Cumberland Presbyterian Church started on the frontier and was well adapted to the task of evangelizing in the new settlements. The early preachers went where the people were, and carried the gospel to those who were without the means of grace. Like Paul they "strived to preach the gospel, not where Christ was named, lest I should build upon another man's foundation." This is why the church spread westward rather than eastward. In 1812 John Carnahan, a licensed Cumberland Presbyterian preacher, moved to Arkansas, and soon afterward was directed to form a circuit on the Arkansas River. In May, 1824, Arkansas Presbytery was constituted. Although the Cumberland Presbyterian Church had been in existence only fifteen years when Sumner Bacon came in contact with it, congregations had been established not only in various parts of Tennessee and Kentucky, but in Alabama, Illinois, Indiana, Missouri, and Arkansas.

\* \* \*

Sumner Bacon applied to the first presbytery he could reach to be ordained and sent as a missionary to Texas, but his request was denied and he was requested to spend a year in study and preparation. Bacon, however, felt that he must go at once, so he arranged all of his affairs at Fayetteville and left for the eastern part of the state of Arkansas to meet a presbytery, but was again refused ordination, though he offered to be examined on the Bible, ancient and modern history, and mathematics. According to McDonnold,* the deciding factors which caused Arkansas Presbytery to reject his plea were his buckskin clothing and the peculiar nature of his call—that it was a call to a special field, a call to preach the gospel in Texas where there were no Protestant ministers.

Bacon, however, was not a man to be discouraged. He went on to Memphis, Tennessee, where he met a number of Cumberland Presbyterians who gave him great encouragement. He also met Rev. Benjamin F.

*McDonnold, *History of the Cumberland Presbyterian Church* p. 264.

Chase, a minister in the Presbyterian Church, who became interested in him and advised him to spend a year as colporteur in Texas. Accordingly, he secured a few Bibles and tracts and, in the latter part of the year 1826, set out for Texas on horseback and came into San Augustine County where he began his work, traveling among the settlements, selling books, and holding prayer meetings. His first sermon was preached under a grove of forest trees near the line of San Augustine and Sabine Counties. In 1831 he taught school on Little Caney, not far from San Augustine.

In the latter part of 1833 or early in 1834, through the instrumentality of the Rev. Mr. Chase above mentioned, Bacon was duly commissioned by the American Bible Society as its **first agent for the Province of Texas.** The following excerpt from the report of the American Bible Society for the year ending May 10, 1834, not only is interesting from the fact of Bacon's appointment, but sheds light upon the situation in Texas religiously:

"To the Province of Texas, in Mexico, a grant of Spanish Bibles and Testaments has been made, and also a few copies in the English tongue. These books were first solicited by our agent in Louisiana, Rev. Benjamin Chase, who made a temporary visit to Texas and found a lamentable destitution of the Scriptures to prevail. Application was soon after made for books by Mr. Sumner Bacon, a resident in the province, who felt deeply anxious that the word of God should there be distributed, and who offered his own services as Agent, even should it be without compensation. He had traveled extensively through the province, and learned the number and moral situation of its inhabitants. 'There are,' he says, 'in the jurisdiction of Nacogdoches, about six hundred American families and three hundred Spanish, and the households destitute of the Bible are as nine to one. Therefore not less than 500 Bibles are wanted immediately towards supplying this jurisdiction alone. In the jurisdictions farther in the interior, where I am also personally acquainted, there are fewer copies of the Word of God in circulation than in this region. . . .' Mr. Bacon, having been recommended by judicious men, as one who would well perform the duties of an Agent, your Board have cheerfully furnished him with a commission."[*]

Bacon continued in this agency until about the time of his visit to the United States in the early part of 1836. During this time he formed two auxiliary societies, one with headquarters at San Augustine, the other at Columbia. **These were the first Bible societies ever organized in Texas.**

Thus far Bacon had been working as a layman, without presbyterial authority. In the year 1835 Mr. Chase learned that a presbytery of the Cumberland Presbyterian Church was to be organized at Alexandria, Louisiana, and urged Bacon to attend. Bacon did so, and was received, licensed, and ordained the same day, the Rev. Mr. Chase preaching the ordination sermon. The licensing and ordaining of a man upon such short notice was such an unusual procedure, that the presbytery spread on its records a statement that this was not to be a precedent for the future.[**]

During the years that Sumner Bacon had been traveling as a lay evangelist and colporteur he had visited all the settlements in the eastern portion of Texas, rendering what spiritual aid he could. He had noticed

*American Bible Society Reports, 18th Report, May 8, 1834, p. 732.
**McDonnold, History of the Cumberland Presbyterian Church, p. 267.

that about seventy-five per cent of the people who came to Texas came over the old San Antonio Trail via Sabine Town, San Augustine, and Nacogdoches. He therefore selected San Augustine as being the best point where he could see the most people coming into the state, and made this his headquarters. With the aid of people then living in San Augustine, he would contact most of the people coming into the country, record their names, make note of their intended destination, tell them of his purposes, and would then visit them on his next trip to the settlements whither they were bound.

Bacon is described by his contemporaries as a man "of rough exterior but possessing a soul of love." Members of his family say he was a man of large frame, a perfect specimen of physical manhood. He was especially prepared for work in Texas at that time. He had lived among the Indians for two years in Arkansas and was well acquainted with their habits. It is said that he often fed them, and many of them became his friends.

During the time when Colonel Bean was land agent for the Mexican government at Nacogdoches, it was reported to Colonel Bean that Bacon's work of preaching and distributing Bibles and tracts would stir up strife among the colonists. Bacon, hearing of this, immediately went to see Colonel Bean, introduced himself, and joked about the combination their names made—Bacon and Bean. With this bit of good humor he got into the good graces of the colonel and was told to go ahead with his work.

Bacon frequently went to Tennessee, which was the center of the Cumberland Presbyterian Church, and on one of these visits, in the early part of the year 1836, he was married at Spring Hill, Maury County, Tennessee, to Miss Elizabeth McKerall. They returned to Texas on horseback. When they arrived in Texas, Santa Anna's invasion was on, so Bacon left his wife at the home of Rev. Samuel Doak McMahon, near the east line of San Augustine County, while he himself hastened to join the Texas army, where he remained until after the battle of San Jacinto. In the meantime he made a trip to New Orleans for General Houston on which he purchased at his own expense thirty-four kegs of powder for the Texas army.[*]

Returning home from the Texas army, Bacon and his wife lived at San Augustine, and the following year bought a home six miles east of San Augustine. Prior to the war for Texas independence, Bacon had not organized any churches, although he had preached in many of the settlements, and had laid a foundation on which to build the Cumberland Presbyterian Church in Texas.

## SHILOH (RED RIVER COUNTY)

In northeastern Texas, adjacent to Red River, is a strip of territory which, during the period of which we write, was still claimed by Arkansas. The treaty between the United States and Spain in connection with the purchase of Florida in 1819 had fixed the east line of Texas as it is now (Texas was then under Spanish dominion), but the line had never been accurately surveyed. This region was represented in

*See Sumner Bacon's letter to Congress of the Republic of Texas, p. 47.

the legislature of Arkansas and also in the convention of Texans which led up to the signing of the declaration of Texas independence. In 1836 when Richard Ellis and A. H. Latimer were representing Red River County in this convention, a son of the former and the father of the latter, who lived in this same region, were members of the Arkansas legislature.

In this section of country, about six miles a little north of east from where the town of Clarksville stands, the first Cumberland Presbyterian Church in Texas was organized by Rev. Milton Estill in the year 1833.* This is believed to have been the first Protestant church of any denomination ever organized in what is now the state of Texas. This congregation was called Shiloh, probably in honor of the Shiloh Cumberland Presbyterian Church in Carroll County, Tennessee, from whence several of its charter members, notably the Latimer family, had come. According to the autobiography of Rev. Richard O. Watkins, who was then a boy seventeen years of age and a charter member of the Shiloh congregation, the first elders were Jesse Watkins (his father) and A. H. Latimer, both of whom had served as elders in the church in Tennessee. Jesse Watkins and his family had been members of the Oak Grove church in McNairy County, Tennessee. The Watkins family settled on what is known as Blossom Prairie, which is

*In giving 1833 as the date of the organization of the Shiloh church, we are aware that the MS. autobiography of Rev. R. O. Watkins places the organization in 1834. The early historians, as well as local tradition, are so unanimous in giving 1833 as the date that we are following them. Rev. R. O. Watkins' autobiography was written more than forty years afterward.

some twenty miles west of where the Shiloh church
was organized, nevertheless they attended the services there.

Among the members of this church were men who
were soon to occupy prominent places in the achievement of Texas independence, for in the convention
held at old Washington in the spring of 1836, where on
March 2 the declaration of Texas independence was
signed, there were three members of the Shiloh Cumberland Presbyterian Church: Richard Ellis, Robert
Hamilton, and Albert Hamilton Latimer. Each of
these men is eulogized at length in S. H. Dixon's
book, The Men Who Made Texas Free. Richard Ellis
not only was a member of the convention and a signer
of the Declaration of Independence, but was elected
chairman and presided over the convention. It was
he for whom Ellis County was named.

The first regular pastor of the Shiloh church was
the Rev. Samuel Corley, who came from Rutherford
County, Tennessee, in the year 1840.* He came up
Red River by boat, landed at old Roland, northeast
of Clarksville, and went through the country to the
home of Rev. James Sampson where he preached his
first sermon in Texas that night, the service having
been announced and the congregation assembled by
runners sent out during the afternoon. Rev. James
Sampson, a school teacher and Cumberland Presbyterian preacher, who had come to Texas in the thir-

*Our information concerning early Cumberland Presbyterian min-
isters in the Clarksville territory is largely drawn from data compiled by the Hon. Pat B. Clark, grandson of the founder of Clarksville and a member of the Stone's Chapel Presbyterian Church,
U. S. A.

ties, lived about five miles northwest of Clarksville, near where the Stone's Chapel Presbyterian Church now stands. Corley ministered for several years to the Shiloh and Savannah churches, and later extended his labors over a wide circuit, which included Paris and Bonham, the counties south of Clarksville, and around to Bowie County. He was not only a great preacher, but also an effective singer. It was said that a hymn sung by Rev. Sam Corley would put any congregation in a worshipful frame of mind.

In about the year 1848 Shiloh and another congregation west of town called Hopewell were consolidated by order of presbytery with the congregation which had been organized in Clarksville. Corley seems to have continued as pastor the greater part of the time until about the year 1857, when he was instrumental in bringing Rev. Amos M. Stone from the presidency of the Female Seminary at McMinnville, Tennessee, who ministered to the Clarksville and other near-by churches for a time. In 1859 Rev. Josiah G. Harris came to Clarksville as pastor. He spent a long ministry in Red River Presbytery. Another minister who had a part in the making of the Clarksville church was Rev. Johnson Dysart, who in 1860 led in the erection of a church building which stood for forty years. The Clarksville congregation continued on as a Cumberland Presbyterian Church until 1906 when under the leadership of Rev. S. M. Templeton, who had been pastor since 1892, this congregation went into the Presbyterian Church, U. S. A.

In the year 1877 another congregation bearing the name Shiloh was organized in the same community where the original Shiloh church had been organized more than forty years before. It is understood from tradition handed down by members of this church that the members of the Cumberland Presbyterian Church who continued to reside in the community, although their names had been transferred to the Clarksville church, soon began again to have services in that community, due to the inconvenience of attending the services regularly in town. However, there is no record of an organization being perfected until the above date. Among the members of this new Shiloh church may be found descendants of some of those who constituted the first Shiloh congregation. A grandson of Robert Hamilton, W. M. Hamilton, served as an elder in this church for many years. Other names prominently connected with this congregation are the Dinwiddies, who came from the old Shiloh church in West Tennessee in 1854, the Fultons, and the Bledsoes. The present location of the Shiloh church is about two miles from where the first Shiloh is said to have been organized. Thus while technically the present Shiloh church may not be able to establish a line of direct continuity from the organization of the older congregation of the same name, this congregation still carries on as a Cumberland Presbyterian church, perpetuating in that community the distinctive tenets of faith on which a group of pioneer Texans, under the leadership of Rev. Milton Estill, organized the first Cumberland Presbyterian congregation in Texas more than a century ago.

Because of the information contained in so short a space regarding personalities who have figured in the history of Cumberland Presbyterianism in Red River County, we quote from an article furnished by Rev.

H. R. Allen who recently had the opportunity of making a rather thorough investigation concerning early Cumberland Presbyterian history in the vicinity of Clarksville, in the course of which he visited the cemetery adjacent to the spot where the old Shiloh church is said to have been located:

"In the cemetery mentioned above I find the following members of the first Cumberland Presbyterian church of Texas, known as Shiloh, were buried: Samuel F. Moore, born 1799, died 1859; Rev. Johnson Dysart, born June 25, 1813, died July 2, 1885; his wife, born August 3, 1816, died August 30, 1862; James Latimer, the father of Albert H. Latimer who was one of the number to attend the convention which led up to the signing of the Declaration of Independence, was born in Connecticut October 15, 1783, came to Texas 1833, and died 1860; his wife, Jane Hamilton Latimer, was born in Guilford County, North Carolina, October 6, 1784, and died April 19, 1855.

"I find connected with this community such men as Rev. Sam Corley, first pastor of the Clarksville church; Rev. James Sampson; Rev. Gilbert Clark, a brother of the James Clark who founded Clarksville, Texas, and which city bears his name, and whose mother was a Cumberland Presbyterian, also; Rev. Amos Stone (Stone's Chapel, about five miles from Clarksville, bears his name); Rev. Johnson Dysart, father of the Rev. E. D. Dysart, so well known to Texas Cumberland Presbyterians during the last thirty or forty years or longer; Rev. Josiah G. Harris; Richard Ellis, who not only was one of the number to sign the Declaration of Independence, but who was chairman of the group who did sign it and who later was given honor by having the county of Ellis named for him."

## TEXAS PRESBYTERY

In the spring of 1836, during the dark days of the struggle of the Texas colonists for freedom from the military despotism of the Mexican government, another young Cumberland Presbyterian minister arrived in Texas. This was Andrew J. McGown, whose father had been a colonel under General Andrew Jackson. McGown's parents had moved to Texas previous to this time, while he remained in the United States attending school in preparation for the ministry, being at the time a licentiate under he care of Mississippi Presbytery. When he heard that Texas had declared her independence he left school and hurried to Texas to cast his lot with his people. He arrived during what was known as the "Great Stampede," when the people of Texas were fleeing before Santa Anna's army. McGown went on and joined the Texas army and participated in the battle of San Jacinto which brought the struggle to a successful termination.

McDonnold credits McGown and Bacon with taking the initiative in the matter of organizing a presbytery in Texas:

"In 1836 McGown and Bacon first met. Both of them had their hearts earnestly set on the interests of Christ's kingdom in the Republic of Texas, for the Lone Star banner then floated over that field. A presbytery, a newspaper, and a school were three things which they agreed to work for. To secure the first they attended the meeting of Mississippi Synod, whose jurisdiction extended indefinitely to the south and west. At their request this synod authorized any three ordained ministers of the Cumberland Presbyterian church who could be got together on Texas soil to organize a presbytery."[*]

On the first page of the minutes of Texas Presbytery we find this resolution as passed by Mississippi

*McDonnold, *History of the Cumberland Presbyterian Church,* p. 268.

Synod in session at Jackon, Mississippi, November 14, 1836:

> "Resolved, that so soon as there may be three or more ministers in the Province of Texas, that they organize themselves into a Presbytery—
>
> "Rev. Sumner Bacon to be their first Moderator and their bounds to include the whole Province."
>
> "Wm. H. Wilkins, Mod.<br>"H. H. Hill, Clk."

McGown was not yet ordained. Estill had returned to Tennessee. There was living in Texas at that time, however, another ordained minister, Rev. Amos Roark, who had been in Texas since 1831 laboring as an evangelist. He had formed a small congregation on Mill Creek in Austin County at the house of James Duff, who had been a member of the Cumberland Presbyterian Church in Tennessee.

During the summer of 1836 Richard O. Watkins, who had moved with his father's family from Red River to Nacogdoches County the year before, surrendered to the call to the ministry. The way seemed dark to him, as there was no presbytery in Texas, and he knew no minister to whom he could go for counsel, but he began studying the only three books he had —his Bible, Ewing's Lectures, and Buck's Theological Dictionary—meanwhile holding services among the people in their homes. In the spring of 1837 Sumner Bacon chanced to pass that way and heard of "the young man who was holding meetings," hunted him up, learned that he too was a Cumberland Presbyterian, and encouraged him, inasmuch as he could not go away to school before the following winter, to begin preaching to the people in the scattered settlements; so, as Bacon had done, Watkins started out without presbyterial authority to hunt up "the scattered, wild, reckless people of Texas and tell them of the salvation of Christ offered freely to all."

Some incidents in Watkins' ministry during this period will serve to illustrate the condition of the people religiously. On arriving in any given settlement, he would inquire as to whose house would be central and who had the most room, and ask the privilege of making an appointment for preaching at their house. Going into a community that did not have a very good reputation for honesty he sought out the leading man of the settlement and asked the liberty of preaching at his house. The man said, "Have you not heard of the bad character of the settlement, and are you not afraid to come here lest your horse be stolen?" Watkins told him that he had heard he was a very bad man and the settlement dangerous to travel through, but he had known of settlements that had been too badly slandered, and he did not believe there was a man mean enough to steal his horse and make him walk to get to his appointments, as his only object was to persuade them to do right and be religious. The man allowed Watkins to hold services in his house, and treated him with the utmost respect.

On another occasion when he had been refused at one house where he had expected to be received cordially, he went on to another house where an old Texan lived who was said to be a refugee from justice, but Watkins adds that "of this it was not considered in good taste to inquire too closely in that day." He visited this family which consisted of the husband and wife and twelve children. None of the children had ever heard a sermon preached, and neither had the parents since they had been in Texas. Watkins made an appointment to preach at their house, and in less than twelve months had the joy of seeing the entire family—father, mother, and twelve children—won to Christ.

In 1837 Rev. Mitchell Smith moved to Texas from Alabama and settled at San Augustine. This made the required three ministers, so arrangements were made for organizing a presbytery. On November 27, 1837, Rev. Sumner Bacon from Louisiana, Mitchell Smith from Talladega, and Amos Roark from Hatchie Presbyteries met at the home of Sumner Bacon, in San Augustine County, and organized a presbytery, which was named Texas Presbytery. Rev. Sumner Bacon served as moderator during the first meeting, and Rev. Mitchell Smith was chosen clerk. Rev. Amos Roark was appointed commissioner to the next General Assembly.

This presbytery entered upon its task bravely. Provision was made for the organization of a home missionary society "for the purpose of supplying the Republic of Texas with the ministry of the Gospel, by the Cumberland Presbyterian Church." The first Monday evening in each month was designated to be observed as "a monthly concert of prayer, for the blessings of God on the cause of missions throughout the world." The presbytery ordered a petition drawn up asking the General Assembly to send missionaries to Texas.

Strong resolutions were adopted enjoining a proper observance of the Sabbath and condemning the "manufacture, use, or traffic of all intoxicating liquors."

The presbytery endorsed the work of the American Bible Society, American Tract Society, American Temperance Union, American Sunday School Union, and several other organizations of a similar nature with headquarters in the United States, and invited them to extend their work to Texas. The prospectus of a non-sectarian religious periodical to be called the "Star of Texas" was endorsed. The presbytery resolved to establish as soon as possible a "seminary of learning" to be conducted on the "manual labor system."

At this meeting Richard O. Watkins presented himself and was received under the care of the presbytery as a candidate for the ministry. His father, Jesse Watkins, had accompanied him to the place of meeting, expecting to attend and assist as a ruling elder in the organization of the presbytery, but when they arrived they found they had come a week too soon, and as the elder Watkins had an appointment to arrange a peace treaty with a group of hostile Indians, he could not remain. He intended, after arranging the treaty with the Indians, to take the Indian delegates to the capital of the republic, make his report and collect his salary, and with the money to send his son, Richard, to school in the United States. With this in view, R. O. Watkins took his letter from the presbytery before its adjournment, but a few days after returning home he learned that his father had been killed by the Indians.

The presbytery adjourned to meet "at Elijah Gossett's on Wednesday before the third Sabbath in September, 1838."

Before the time arrived for the next meeting, however, the following call was issued:

"Moderator's Call—To the ministers and Church Sessions, of the Texas Pres. of the C. P. Church.

"Dear Brethren:

"I find it necessary for our Pres. to meet sooner than the time to which it stands adjourned; therefore with the advice of several of the brethren, and by authority of the Constitution, in cases of Emergency, I do hereby call the Texas Pres. to meet in the town of San Augustine, Republic of Texas, on Saturday the 1st day of Sept., 1838, to transact certain business which will **then** and **there** be made known.

"This 20th day of August A.D. 1838.
"Sumner Bacon, Mod."

When presbytery convened, the moderator informed the presbytery "that in consequence of the late insurrection and war in the country it was necessary to remove the fall session of presbytery from the Trinidad to some other place and time." Rev. R. O. Watkins, in his autobiography, states that the settlement where presbyery was to meet had been "entirely broken up by hostile Indians."

Bethel meeting house, San Augustine County, where a Presbyterian Church had been established, was selected as the place, and Friday the 14th of September as the time. At this called meeting Rev. James McDonnold from New Lebanon Presbytery, Rev. Samuel W. Frazier from Jackson Presbytery, and Licentiate Andrew J. McGown from Mississippi Presbytery were received by letter. Candidate R. O. Watkins returned his letter and was taken under the care of the presbytery.

The second regular meeting, held at Bethel meeting house, was attended by the five ordained ministers, Licentiate McGown, and Candidate Watkins. Rev.

James McDonnold was moderator and Rev. S. W. Frazier clerk.

William Sansom, a licentiate, was received by letter from the Methodist Protestant Church and his acceptance of the Confession of Faith of the Cumberland Presbyterian Church. Enoch Jones was received under the care of presbytery as a candidate for the ministry. (The latter was dropped from the roll at the next meeting.)

The following item is reminiscent of pre-Civil War days:

> "Charles Polk's colored man, Tennessee, petitioned the presbytery for leave to exercise his gift in reading the Scriptures, singing, prayer and exhortation among his colored friends, and having produced testimonials of his good moral conduct; of his communion in the church; and the presbytery having examined him as to his experimental acquaintance with religion; as to his internal impressions and the motives which induced him to desire this liberty— with Mr. Polk's consent, his petition was granted."

At this meeting R. O. Watkins was licensed to preach the gospel, **the first minister of any Protestant denomination to be licensed on Texas soil.**

Rev. Amos Roark made his report as commissioner to the last General Assembly. Rev. Samuel W. Frazier, whom the Assembly had sent as a missionary to Texas, had accompanied Roark home, holding meetings on the way. At this meeting he was recognized as the General Assembly's missionary, and directed "to visit the principal towns and neighborhoods in our bounds and collect the scattered members of our church, and organize congregations where he may deem expedient, and to do all he can in favor of Sabbath Schools and the cause of Temperance."

At this meeting the plan of forming extensive circuits to supply the means of grace to the sparsely inhabited settlements, which had been so widely used in the early days of the Cumberland Presbyterian Church farther east, was officially introduced into Texas. Rev. Amos Roark was ordered to form a circuit between main Red River and the Sulphur Fork, to be called the "Clarksville Circuit," while Licentiate R. O. Watkins was directed to preach on a circuit "which he shall form West of the Attoyac, and east of the Neches, to be known as the Nacogdoches Circuit." The other ministers of the presbytery, Revs. McDonnold, Bacon, Smith, and Sansom, were ordered to "labor industriously in the ministry, **at least every Sabbath,** until the next stated session of this Presbytery." (Those who were riding the circuit would likely preach almost every day.)

In the fall of 1838 there was a great deal of trouble with the Indians in east Texas who were being incited by the Mexican population of that section. These Mexicans, of whom there were quite a number in Nacogdoches County, were not wholly satisfied with the separation of Texas from Mexico. The danger and confusion was such that R. O. Watkins, who was preaching in the section where the trouble was greatest, was forced to give up the idea of preaching regularly for the time being, and joined a company of rangers for the protection of the people he was preaching to. This trouble culminated in the famous Kickapoo fight in which General Rusk with his minute men gained a decisive victory over the Indians and Mexicans and drove them farther back into the wilderness.

Although Watkins could not preach in the settlements where he had intended, he did preach to the rangers, and by his integrity, his participation with them in their innocent amusements, and his readiness to take part in any danger to which duty called, won for himself a warm place in the hearts of this company of rangers.

On one occasion a courier rode into camp bearing a message from the colonel forty miles away, which necessitated an immediate reply. As the hour was growing late, the courier refused to undertake the dangerous task of taking the dispatch to the colonel. The captain called for a volunteer, but all hesitated. Watkins spoke to one of his comrades, James H. Sparks, who in after years became an elder in the Cumberland Presbyterian Church, and asked, "Will you bear me company if I will volunteer?" Sparks finally consented, and the two set out with nothing to guide them through the darkness of the night except the direction of a light breeze which was blowing. When the wind lay so that they could not tell its direction in any other way, they did so by putting the finger in the mouth for a moment until it was warm, then holding it up to see which side cooled first. Thus they kept their course, and before morning reached a point known to both and twenty miles away from where they had started.

They had thought themselves to be out of danger, but suddenly found themselves within twenty yards of an Indian camp fire. They saw that they were discovered, so they decided the boldest course was best, and with the cry of "Charge, charge!" as though the whole company were there, they dashed boldly toward the fire while the Indians scattered every way, and so went by at full speed and concluded the trip in safety.

The third regular meeting of Texas Presbytery was convened in San Augustine March 14, 1839. Rev. Milton Moore was present at this meeting and was received by letter from Hatchie Presbytery. The presbytery was deeply affected over the loss of Rev. Samuel W. Frazier who had died the fall before, after he had been in Texas only a few months. At the time of his death he was serving as chaplain of the Senate of the Republic of Texas.

McGown was directed to prepare for ordination at the next meeting. Before the time arrived, however, he had returned to the States, and was ordained there, returning to Texas as an ordained minister a few years later.

The nature of the work assigned to the various ministers for the ensuing six months may be seen from the following:

"Ordered that J. McDonnold, S. Bacon, M. Smith, and M. Moore preach one Sabbath in each month: J. McDonnold, to Bear Creek and Hopewell, and the rest of his time where he may think best; S. Bacon at San Augustine and Hopewell; M. Smith at Hopewell, McMaham Mills, and Clark's on the Polygocha; M. Moore at Nacogdoches and in the vicinity, until the next stated session of this Presbytery.

"Ordered that the ordained ministers belonging to this Presbytery report all conversions, accessions and baptisms.

"Ordered that Amos Roark preach until the next stated session of this Presbytery when and where he may think will be most conducive to God's glory and the advancement of the Redeemer's Kingdom in the bounds of this Republic and that he make collections for his support, and do all he can to form societies, instruct the youth and ascertain as

Believed to be a likeness
of
REV. SUMNER BACON

MRS. SUMNER BACON
Born March 29, 1810
Died November 30, 1879

REV. AND MRS. MITCHELL
SMITH

Mitchell Smith was the first stated clerk of Texas Presbytery; Mrs. Smith cooked for the first presbytery, which concluded its meeting in their home.

REV. RICHARD OVERTON
WATKINS

First Protestant minister ordained in Texas

far as he can the numerical strength of our church in the Republic."

Presbytery adjourned to meet at Hopewell meeting house in September following.

Soon after this the idea of forming a church organization independent of the church in the United States began to be talked, as some felt that inasmuch as Texas was an independent republic it should have its own church, and on account of the great distance it would be impossible to attend the General Assembly in the United States.* In the spring of 1840, the presbytery met in Nacogdoches County near the home of R. O. Watkins, and although some two or three ministers opposed it, a resolution was passed asking Mississippi Synod to rescind the order creating the presbytery. This procedure was taken because it was thought any other means of withdrawal would indicate a rebellious spirit. That fall the presbytery met at Fort Houston, in what is now Anderson County, to consummate the organization, but for some reason the matter was postponed. At the next meeting it was again postponed, and in the fall of 1841, in session at Melrose, Nacogdoches County, near the home of Rev. Milton Moore, the subject of an independent organization was dropped entirely, and resolutions were passed looking toward the formation of a synod.

It was at the meeting held at Fort Houston in the fall of 1840 that Rev. R. O. Watkins was ordained. **He was the first minister of any Protestant denomination to be ordained on Texas soil.** To this meeting of

*Crisman's *Origin and Doctrines of the Cumberland Presbyterian Church.*

presbytery the members coming from eastern Texas traveled in a body, on account of danger from Indians. While Watkins was engaged late one evening in preparing his trial sermon which he was to preach that night preparatory to ordination, his horse got away, and he was faced with the necessity of walking home, a distance of almost one hundred miles. Watkins, however, preached that night to the satisfaction of the presbytery, and the next day was ordained. Rev. Milton Estill who had organized the first Cumberland Presbyterian church in Texas, preached the ordination sermon and Sumner Bacon delivered the charge. When the time came to go home, a man who had been out on an Indian hunt came along with a lead horse going Watkins' way, and tendered him the use of the horse, by which he reached the first stage of his journey, and by walking part of the way, then obtaining another horse, he reached home in safety.

The year 1841 was characterized by a number of great revivals. In one camp meeting alone, that held at Douglass, which was one of R. O. Watkins' appointments, there were seventy-five conversions. The hands of the presbytery were further strengthened during 1840 and 1841 by the arrival of Rev. Samuel Corley and the Revs. John M. and Finis E. Foster. That fall the presbytery memorialized Mississippi Synod to divide the presbytery into three presbyteries, and requested the General Assembly to establish the Texas Synod.

The two new presbyteries were Colorado Presbytery, which included everything west of the Trinity River, and Red River Presbytery, which lay between the Sabine and Red Rivers.

The first meeting of Red River Presbytery was held at Clarksville in December, 1842. The ministers who composed it were James Sampson, Samuel Corley, and John McKee. The first act of this presbytery was to call for candidates for the ministry, whereupon Gilbert Clark, brother of James Clark who founded Clarksville, came forward and was received and licensed to preach the gospel.* Colorado Presbytery was organized March 28, 1843.** The original members of this presbytery were Milton Estill, Finis E. Foster, A. J. McGown, and Robert Gilkerson.

## TEXAS SYNOD ORGANIZED

Texas Synod was organized near Nacogdoches in 1843. A camp meeting was held in conjunction with the meeting of synod. Congregations at this meeting were large and "so impressive was the divine influence," says Watkins, "that it appeared almost impossible for anyone to remain long on the ground without being the subject of feelings of deep solemnity." A number of army officers and professional men came to these meetings. They expressed their skepticism concerning what was going on, and sought to account for all of the manifestations of divine power as being caused by excitement. They had so expressed themselves to Rev. Sam Corley, who as it happened was to preach that night. When Corley mounted the stand and had read a hymn, he stated that he was going to change the order of things tonight; that he wished for all of those who were anxiously seeking religion to

*According to Hon. Pat B. Clark, Clarksville, Texas.

**The Cumberland Presbyterian, vol. 56, p. 984.

come to the front now instead of after the sermon. About sixty came, and after Corley had counted their number, he turned to the gentlemen referred to and asked them to see for themselves that there was no excitement there. At the close of the sermon when he extended the invitation, a large number came forward, and more than fifty found salvation that night. Among the number was Mrs. Mary Rusk, wife of General Rusk.

"Here," Watkins tells us, "he (Watkins) met Rev. Sumner Bacon for the last time. Bacon had earnestly desired and prayed that he might see a synod organized in Texas. After the business was done he said that he had assurance satisfactory that his work was done, that he had now but to get home and die. After the declaration of Bacon that he would meet no more, he received the last counsel of that eminent pioneer preacher of Texas, and with deep sympathy received the last blessing and mantle 'as his Texas Boy,' of this faithful servant of God."

## MINISTERS AND CHURCHES OF THE FIRST PRESBYTERY

Of all of those who had a part in planting the Cumberland Presbyterian Church in Texas, Sumner Bacon is rightfully recognized as the pioneer who blazed the trail. The first to catch the vision of the work to be done by the Cumberland Presbyterian Church in the transformation of this great wilderness of the Southwest, his whole ministerial life was given to the work in Texas, and he lived just long enough to see his dreams come into fruition. His ministerial work was principally in the extreme eastern portion of the state, but his influence was felt over the whole Republic of Texas. Dr. W. S. Red, in his book, The Texas Colonists and Religion, says of him: "In history of Protestantism in Colonial Texas, Sumner Bacon occupies a place that can be accorded to no other. That which Francis McKamie was to the American Colonists Sumner Bacon was to the Texas Colonists. His consecrated life shows that he was moved by the same spirit that made Paul the apostle to the Gentiles." Bacon died January 24, 1844, then only fifty-four years of age, but with the witness in his own heart that his work was finished. He was buried near his home, five miles east of San Augustine in Chapel Hill Cemetery.

Mitchell Smith was living at San Augustine when the first meeting of Texas Presbytery was held. After the presbytery was convened, it was moved, on account of Mrs. Bacon's illness, to Mitchell Smith's house, which consisted of a single log room, and when it became necessary to cook a meal, the presbytery moved out into the yard, where a large pine log was used for a writing table. Smith afterward moved to Panola County where he spent many years in the ministry.

Amos Roark remained in Texas only a few years, but during that time his ministry extended to all parts of the Republic. In the winter of 1839-40 he was living in Austin, and in January, 1840, spent two days in taking what was probably the first census of this the capital of Texas, which at that time had a population of 856 souls. Roark returned to the United States in 1840 or 1841.

Milton Estill, who organized the first Cumberland Presbyterian church in Texas in 1833 and returned to

Tennessee soon after, came back to Texas in about the year 1840 and spent the remainder of his life here. He spent a long ministry in south central Texas, and died April 28, 1882, near Dodge, in Walker County.

Andrew J. McGown labored principally in south central Texas, but more or less all over the state. Wherever he went his comrades of the days of the Texas revolution would rally around him, and he was the means of leading many of them to Christ. In 1846 he established the first Cumberland Presbyterian newspaper in Texas, The Texas Presbyterian, which he published until 1857, files of which are preserved in the library of the University of Texas.

R. O. Watkins, the first minister of any denomination to be licensed and ordained in Texas, preached in the vicinity of Nacogdoches for many years, and later, about the year 1855, moved to Kemp, Kaufman County, where he made his home the greater part of the time during the remainder of his life. A charter member of the first Cumberland Presbyterian church ever organized in Texas, he was present also at the first presbytery and the first synod, and attended the General Assembly in 1845 bearing the request of the synod that the General Assembly recognize the organization of the synod as valid even though the required number of presbyteries were not represented at its first meeting. Though often having to battle against ill health, Watkins covered an extensive territory with his ministry. He was frequently called upon to travel in the general interest of the church in his presbytery and synod. He passed to his reward May 27, 1897, after a ministry of more than sixty years, all of it spent in Texas.

A few words might well be said concerning the educational qualifications of these men. They were in the class of what we would call self-made men. They did not hold theological degrees, but as a result of study and experience they were educated men. Even though Watkins had only three books when he began studying for the ministry, we may be sure that he attained a thorough knowledge of what was in them. Through perseverance he did secure a well-rounded education. Bacon had no theological training, although he was well trained in other fields. He is said to have been a fine historian and a splendid mathematician. Watkins was a staunch friend of Trinity University. He had always advocated the establishing of one central institution of learning for the church in Texas, rather than the policy of each presbytery or synod attempting to maintain a separate school. To aid in the endowment of that institution he turned over to it a section of land which he had received for his services to the Republic of Texas.

A fine spirit of cooperation existed between the Cumberland Presbyterians and ministers of other evangelical denominations, as has usually been the case with Cumberland Presbyterians. Bacon held his first camp meeting with a Methodist preacher by the name of Barnett. The second regular meeting of presbytery was held in a Presbyterian church. James Burke, a Presbyterian elder who was present at the first meeting, was seated as a corresponding member and rendered valuable assistance.

Let us not make the mistake of supposing, however, that these men minimized the doctrinal principles upon which their own church stood, or that they would have sacrificed its teachings regarding the plan of salvation which came to be known as the medium theology. In fact, the records show that they labored with a consciousness that the Cumberland Presbyterian Church had a God-given mission.

As an illustration, R. O. Watkins was on his way to the United States to attend school. In company with Sumner Bacon, who was going to Mississippi, he stopped over at Natchez and attended a presbytery of the Presbyterian Church, where he met Rev. Benjamin Chase and other noted ministers. The president of one of their colleges sought to induce him to attend school there, but before he made up his mind to do so, he heard a young candidate for the ministry read a discourse on the subject of the atonement, in which he took the position that all for whom atonement was made would certainly be called, regenerated, and saved. This was fully approved by the presbytery, and the candidate was licensed on the strength of it. This was so different from his view of things that Watkins decided he should go where a different theology from that was taught.

The records of the first presbytery show that much attention was given to the task of hunting up the Cumberland Presbyterians in the scattered settlements and forming them into congregations, a work which in our own day is yet unfinished.

These ministers labored for the most part without salary and had to make their living by the work of their own hands. Bacon did not make tents as did Paul, but he made turpentine. His place lay partly in the long-leaf pine region, and he made the first turpentine that was ever made west of the Mississippi River.

Even after the churches became stronger and more numerous, many of them were slow to accept their responsibility for supporting the ministry of the Word. R. O. Watkins' churches at one time urged him to devote his full time to the ministry, promising that they would at least pay the wages of a hand to take his place on the farm. "The hand was hired," Watkins says, "and he (Watkins) extended his labors into Shelby County, but unfortunately the hand had to be paid out of the proceeds of his own little farm."

Not much data of a definite nature exists from which to reconstruct the history of the congregations which made up the first presbytery, except that of Shiloh (Red River County) which has already been given. The Committee on State of Religion, appointed at the second stated meeting of presbytery, reported that there were at that time five organized churches with a total membership of about 90. Bacon had organized a church near his home in San Augustine County in the summer of 1836, and in the same year established a camp ground where meetings were held regularly for twenty years. The exact date of the organization of the Nacogdoches church is not known, but it was partially organized in the historic old stone house in the town, and later (about 1840) moved out four miles north to the neighborhood where Watkins lived. Watkins also preached at Douglass, sixteen miles west from where he lived, and organized a church there at a very early day. Dr. Crisman, in the appendix to his Origin and Doctrines, says that "by this time (1842) several congregations had been organized on the Colorado and Guadalupe Rivers, and flourishing congregations had been established in the Red River country."

## BACON'S LETTER TO CONGRESS

Because of what it reveals as to the part this pioneer preacher had in helping to bring about the achievement of Texas independence, we quote the following letter which, in Bacon's own handwriting, is filed with the archives of the Republic of Texas in the state capitol. This was written just a few months before Bacon's death. The debt was never paid.

The Republic of Texas
County of San Augustine

To the Hon Senate and House of Representatives in Congress Assembled.

The petition of Sumner Bacon, a citizen of the County of San Augustine, humbly complaining, unto the Honorable Congress most respectfully represents that in the latter part of March or First of April A.D. 1836 he purchased in the City of New Orleans thirty four (34) Kegs of powder, weighing fifty lbs. each which cost thirty three (33) cents per pound; making five hundred and sixty one dollars (561.00) the original cost. And petitioner further represents that said powder was delivered over to M. Bryany the Texas agent to purchase supplies of ammunition, munitions of war and etc.; and by him was shipped on board the schooner Congress and was received at Matagorda and was made use of for the benefit of Texas during her struggle for Independence in the year A.D. 1836. All of which petitioner is ready to verify. And petitioner further shows that he has never received one cent by way of compensation for said powder purchased by him as aforesaid, nor for his time, trouble and expense in making, the purchase; that in doing of it, he was prompted by the love of the country, the purest motives and a desire to assist and contribute his mite to the support of the war, then pending for

National Independence, and with a knowledge that the Government was at that time poor and unable to pay and perhaps never would be.

Petitioner shows that these were the motives by which he was actuated; and others actuated by less patriotic motives, assisted the Government in a similar manner and have long since been amply remunerated.

Petitioner represents (as is well known) that he is a poor man and has to support a large family by the work of his own hands, and is unable to sustain the loss of the five hundred sixty-one dollars and to contribute so largely to the welfare of the body politic. He has laid out of the use of his money for seven years, and waited patiently, until the country was relieved from and able to compensate him. He believes that period has arrived, and therefore asks that remuneration and compensation to which justice and equity would justly entitle him, and as may seem right and proper to the Honorable Congress from the foregoing premises. Your petitioner would further represent that in the year 1842, a similar petition to this was presented to the Hon. Congress when in session at Austin, and has not been heard from since, and consequently petitioner thought it proper to present a second, containing the same facts and lest the Congress should again be convened at Washington or elsewhere.

The foregoing acts contained in this petition are humbly submitted, by petitioner, to the consideration of the Honorable Congress, to whom I have to look as my only source of redress, and from whom I shall confidently expect (I shall patiently wait the result) that relief to which justice will entitle me. As in duty bound will ever pray, etc.

                              Sumner Bacon
                              Petitioner

San Augustine, Nov. 9, 1843

## Chapter II

# PLANTING THE CHURCH IN A GROWING
# COUNTRY

## (1843-1869)

FOR several years the new synod underwent a struggle for existence. Although immigrants continued to pour into Texas, there were few preachers among them. Those who were here labored under many hardships. The unsettled state of the country, due to Indian depredations in the new settlements, internal disturbances, and the fact that the government in Mexico had never recognized the independence of Texas, made the task of establishing churches a difficult one.

In 1844 there occurred in Shelby County what was known as the war between the Regulators and the Moderators. Those who styled themselves Regulators had formed a company which undertook to take the law into their own hands and rid the country of certain alleged undesirables. They were opposed by another party who called themselves Moderators. The feud became so intense that it is said men were being murdered almost every day. Finally, President Houston had to call out the militia to restore order. Rev. R. O. Watkins, who was then preaching in Shelby County, preached sometimes to friends of one party and sometimes to friends of the other, which made his task a very delicate one, but he so conducted himself that he kept the respect and good will of both parties, although a battle was fought at one of his church houses and a number to whom he had been preaching were killed.

On February 19, 1846, Texas became a state of the

United States by process of annexation. This assured the protection of a stronger government, and gave a new impetus to immigration. During the next few years the state settled up rapidly. Among the new settlers were many Cumberland Presbyterians from Tennessee, Alabama, Missouri, Arkansas, Mississippi, and other states. A number of our strongest churches had their origin in the period from 1847 to the outbreak of the Civil War.

## EARLY CHURCHES IN RUSK COUNTY—THE HAMILTONS*

The first Cumberland Presbyterian church which was organized in what is now Rusk County was at Henderson in 1845. The elders elected at the organization of this church were Andrew Hamilton, Andrew Roberson, and "Uncle Jimmie" Cameron. Rev. R. O. Watkins was the first pastor of this church, which was then in Nacogdoches County.

A few years later a church was organized about five miles west of Henderson and was known as Pleasant Hill, where records show that services were being held in 1856 and 1857. This church was built on land donated by Robert Smith and wife, Mrs. Mary Watkins Smith, sister of Rev. R. O. Watkins. Andrew Hamilton was clerk of the session.

In 1858 or 1859 a church was organized at London, ten miles northwest of Henderson. The elders in this church were James S. Hamilton and James B. Dobbins.

*From data furnished by Mrs. Alice Hamilton Florence Grissom, and biography of Rev. Y. H. Hamilton by his daughter, Mrs. Dollie Hamilton Forester.

They were loyal to the church, and loved and labored with men of all denominations for the salvation of souls, and London was at one time one of the strong churches in this section of the country. Rev. D. C. Nevills was the first pastor.

The Mt. Hope church was organized in 1860, its original location being about two miles nearer Henderson than its present location. Among the early pastors of this church were Revs. Y. H. Hamilton and A. S. Hayter. Among the charter members of this church was John H. Henson who, three years later at the age of eighteen, was made a ruling elder and served as such until his death in 1932. When oil was discovered in the community in 1931, the town of Joinerville sprang up almost overnight. Mt. Hope being the only church in that immediate community, through the efforts of Mr. Henson, his daughter, Mrs. W. H. Stroud, and a few other faithful members and friends of the church, a large number of the new residents of the community were brought into the Sunday school and eventually into the church. Mt. Hope now supports a pastor full time, has one of the most beautiful modest church buildings to be found, and the Sunday school, which has been in existence continuously since 1872, has a regular attendance of around two hundred.

Another congregation organized in the early days of Rusk County was Pine Grove, which was located about a mile from where the town of Overton now is. Where the town now stands there was nothing but a country road and a race track. The elders in this church were J. S. Hamilton, Fed Gipson, and A. Robertson. With the coming of the I&GN Railroad in 1872, this congregation moved to Overton, and Harve McKay and Dr. C. P. Eskridge were added to the eldership. Later, due to the death and removal of most of its members, this church disbanded, and the plot of ground where the old church stood was lost sight of. A few years ago a Cumberland Presbyterian lady who had moved into Overton and knew of the old church which once had been there began to inquire about the location of the old church property. The site was found, and under the leadership of Rev. G. F. Harris a church was organized in 1926 and a new building erected on the old location.

We have seen how closely interwoven with the early history of the Cumberland Presbyterian Church in Rusk County is that of the family of Andrew Hamilton, who was himself a charter member in the first Cumberland Presbyterian church ever organized in that county. Andrew Hamilton was born in Union County, South Carolina, in 1794, served under General Andrew Jackson in the war of 1812, moved to Tennessee in 1825, and thence to Texas. General James Smith, who was a brother-in-law to Hamilton, had come to Texas in 1833. In the latter part of 1834, Hamilton, with his own family, Smith's family, and several others, set out to join General Smith, and with their household goods, slaves and live stock came by boat to Nachitoches, Louisiana, where they landed, loaded their household goods, and all who could not walk, into wagons drawn by oxen, horses and mule teams, and started overland to Nacogdoches, arriving in Texas on the first day of January, 1835. After spending one year in the village of Nacogdoches, Hamilton and Smith settled on adjoining farms where the town of Henderson now stands.

When the trouble with Mexico broke out, General Smith returned to Tennessee and Alabama and raised a company of volunteers, seventy-five in number, to help fight for Texas freedom, while Hamilton remained to look after the families and interests of both. Smith returned with his company, enlisted them in the service, and they were mustered out in September, 1836, after Texas had won her independence. The entire expense of this company of volunteers was borne jointly by Andrew Hamilton and General Smith.

The Hamiltons had been Presbyterians in South Carolina and Tennessee, but cast their lot with the Cumberland Presbyterian Church when a church of that denomination was organized at Henderson. Andrew Hamilton and wife reared a family of nine children, all of whom were baptized and received into the church by Rev. R. O. Watkins, affectionately known as "Uncle Dick." Three sons—James S. Hamilton, Jack Hamilton, and Dr. Andrew Hamilton—became elders in the Cumberland Presbyterian Church, and another son, Young Harrington Hamilton, became a minister.

James S. Hamilton was the father of Mrs. Alice Grissom, who after her removal from the London community to Overton, initiated the move to locate the old church property and re-establish the Cumberland Presbyterian Church in Overton.

Rev. Y. H. Hamilton, who was born in 1828 while the family was living in Tennessee, was converted at the age of eighteen under the ministry of Rev. Finis Foster, joined Texas Presbytery in 1854, and was ordained the following year. He spent the first eight years of his ministerial life in Texas Presbytery and served the following congregations in Rusk and adjoining counties: London, Lynn Flat, Mount Tabor, Princeton, Pine Grove, and Mt. Hope. In 1863 he moved to Grand View, Johnson County, where he and his wife were the first teachers of Rock Hill Academy, one of the earliest cultural centers of that county. In 1866 he moved to Hill County, locating near Woodbury, where he made his home until his death in 1880, meanwhile ministering to churches at Grandview, Friendship, Aquilla, Peoria, Hillsboro, Milford, Oak Grove, Whitney, Brushy Knob, and Clifton.

## MINISTERS IN TEXAS PRESBYTERY

Rev. Clemens Means* came to Texas from Sparta Presbytery (Tennessee) in 1848 and settled in Nacogdoches County. He preached his first sermon in Texas at the home of Alfred Tate. Soon afterward he took charge of the churches at Rockspring and Douglass, to which churches he preached monthly for thirty years. He also preached at Carreso and Friendship. When he arrived in Texas he found two of his old friends and former associates in the ministry who had come to Texas before him: James McDonnold and James S. Guthrie. He and Guthrie joined Texas Presbytery at the same time in the summer of 1849. At that time the following ministers composed Texas Presbytery: James McDonnold, J. C. Barnett, R. O. Watkins, A. H. Watkins, Mitchell Smith, Robert Gilkerson, Ruter, and Cunningham.

Rev. A. S. Hayter came to Texas in 1851 and also settled in Nacogdoches County. He, also, had been associated with Clemens Means in Tennessee. When Rev.

*From autobiography of Rev. Clemens Means in *Our Old Men*, Vol. i, by E. B. Crisman.

Rev. Young Harrington
Hamilton

Rev. A. H. (Arch)
Watkins

R. O. Watkins moved farther west, A. S. Hayter succeeded him on his old charge in Nacogdoches County.

Means' ministry in Texas was confined to Nacogdoches, Angelina, Shelby, San Augustine, and Rusk Counties. While other ministers who came to Texas went farther west to what appeared to be more promising fields, he remained in Texas Presbytery helping to keep alive the work of his church in this the cradle of Cumberland Presbyterianism in Texas.

### PINE TREE

The Pine Tree Cumberland Presbyterian Church, which is located about five miles west of Longview in what was at the time of its organization the southeastern portion of Upshur County, was organized by Rev. Solomon Awalt on October 10, 1847, with fifteen charter members: John Rodden, Mrs. Amelia Rodden, J. T. Echols, Mrs. Martha Echols, Mrs. Ann E. Awalt, Jessie Freeze, Margaret Freeze, James B. White, J. W. Barnes, A. T. Castleberry, and Mrs. Elmira Castleberry (for whom Elmira Chapel was afterward named). The first elders were John Rodden and J. T. Echols.

According to the local tradition, the organization was effected in the open forest, services being held in the shade of growing timber under and around a large pine, from which the church got its name, Pine Tree. A schoolhouse was built on the hill, just north of the old spring, and was used for religious services for a number of years. Later a log church building was erected, which served as a house of worship until 1858, the date given by a number of people for the building of the hexagon shaped frame building which stood for

Rev. Solomon Awalt
Pastor of Pine Tree
Church, 1847 to 1872

Rev. S. R. Chadick, D.D.
First teacher in Chapel
Hill College, Dain-
gerfield

PINE TREE CHURCH, NEAR LONGVIEW, TEXAS
1858-1932

NEW CHURCH AT PINE TREE, ERECTED 1932

seventy-four years. In 1932 a brick and tile building was erected.

Rev. Solomon Awalt, the pioneer preacher of the community, was pastor from 1847 to 1872. Other pastors who have served this church include Revs. S. R. Chadick, W. M. Allen, W. B. Allen, J. H. Robinson, W. V. McGhee, W. R. Edwards, A. W. Yell, R. S. Garrett, B. E. Bowmer, and W. R. Harber, the present pastor, who served from 1910 to 1916 and again from 1926 until the present, and under whose ministry Pine Tree has become a full time pastorate.

For eighty-nine years Pine Tree has carried on, with a membership ranging from fifteen to one hundred and fifty. This church had established a reputation for its loyal support of the denominational benevolences long before the discovery of oil, and now that some of its members have been so fortunate as to benefit in a substantial way from this underground wealth, it has been proved that "he that is faithful in that which is least is faithful also in much."

## THE MARSHALL CHURCH

A recent year book of the Marshall church contains the following information regarding the early history of that congregation:

"The Cumberland Presbyterian Church of Marshall, Texas, was organized April 11, 1848. James Rogers, Margaret Rogers, D. K. Fisher, Julia B. Fisher, Stephen G. Fisher, Alexander Rothy, G. R. Thompson, B. F. Young, Mary Thompson, Elizabeth Rogers, Isabelle Craig, Rev. F. H. Sibley, J. C. Craig, Sarah Irwin, Johnson McClaran, Samuel McClaran, Elijah Blackwell, and Mrs. Blackwell were the charter members. The first ruling elders were

James Rogers, B. F. Young, D. R. Fisher, and Eli Craig.

"On May 16, 1848, nine members were received into the church and of these Judge Joseph Mason was added to the session and made clerk.

"Rev. James Sampson' preached occasionally for the new organization until January, 1850, at which time Rev. Thomas Wilson, D.D., came to Marshall from Leighton, Alabama, to take up the duties of president of the Marshall Masonic Institute. Dr. Wilson was soon elected pastor, and thankfully accepted the offer of the Baptist people, who had the only house of worship in Marshall, to use their building. The two denominations worshiped together with great fraternal harmony.

"Mrs. M. J. Maulding, who joined the church in 1849, reported that the house of worship was built in 1851, and dedicated in 1852.

"In about 1852, Dr. E. P. M. Johnson came to Marshall, and having belonged to Dr. Wilson's church in Alabama, he united with the Cumberland Presbyterian Church of Marshall and was made a ruling elder, which office he held until the day of his death.

"Dr. Wilson was a great believer in revivals, and the membership increased rapidly under his ministry. On June 22, 1873, he passed to his reward, having been pastor of the Marshall Cumberland Presbyterian Church for twenty-three years."

Rev. James Sampson had been appointed by synod in 1847 to missionary work in Harrison County,* and this church seems to have been the result of his labors. Among the charter members we note the names of Fisher and McClaran which are familiar today because of their connection with the work of the Cumberland Presbyterian Church in and around Marshall. (There are sixteen descendants of Johnson McClaran in the Hope Chapel congregation alone.)

*Crisman, Origin and Doctrines.

REV. THOMAS B. WILSON,
D.D.
Pastor of Marshall
Church 1850 to
1873

REV. W. T. INGRAM
Pastor of Marshall
Church since 1925

MARSHALL C. P. CHURCH, ERECTED IN 1932

Soon after Dr. Wilson came to Marshall he organized another congregation about ten miles south of Marshall which was known as Ewing Chapel, and served the Marshall and Ewing Chapel congregations as one charge. Later the Marshall church became a full time pastorate, and Ewing Chapel was served by other ministers of the Marshall Presbytery. This congregation was later moved from its original location about two miles east to what is known as the Gill community, but the old church building still stands on its original site, one of the landmarks of Harrison County.

Under the leadership of the various pastors who have served the Marshall church since Dr. Wilson's time, that congregation has been maintained on a substantial basis and has made its contribution to the moral and religious life of the town. Among the high points in the history of this congregation is a great revival conducted by Dr. R. G. Pearson during the pastorate of Rev. Jerry Ward (1879-1888). This revival, which started in the Cumberland Presbyterian Church, was later moved to the opera house to accommodate the great numbers of people who came to hear his wonderful messages. There were two hundred and eighty-two professions, and seventy accessions to the Cumberland Presbyterian Church, as a result of this revival. The administration of the present pastor, Rev. W. T. Ingram, who became pastor in February, 1925, has been an eminently successful one from several standpoints. Under his leadership the new modern church plant was erected in 1932. There has been a substantial increase in membership under his ministry. This congregation now has a membership of about two hundred, with a Sunday school enrollment of about the same number.

The Hope Chapel congregation had its origin in a protracted meeting held at Hope schoolhouse, about three and a half miles south of town, by Rev. H. F. Bone, D.D., while he was pastor of the Marshall church, and was first organized on August 20, 1889, as a branch of the Marshall church. Two years later it was received as a separate congregation. Early in its history this congregation was led to see the value of having a resident pastor and built a manse, and under the ministry of the various pastors who have made this their home, Hope Chapel has become one of our outstanding rural churches in Texas.

In about the year 1900 another church was organized northwest of town, known as Nesbitt. In 1911 the Hope Chapel congregation divided, about half of the membership withdrawing to build a church at Fairview, one and a half miles east on the Carthage highway. Thus it will be seen that from its beginning with the organization of the Marshall church eighty-eight years ago, the Cumberland Presbyterian Church has made substantial progress in the Marshall territory, and is a vital force for good in the various communities where it is represented.

## NEW PRESBYTERIES IN EAST TEXAS

A fourth presbytery, bearing the name Trinity Presbytery, was created in 1845, embracing the territory between the Angelina and Trinity Rivers. At the meeting of synod which was held at Marshall in 1848 two more presbyteries, Marshall and Frazier, were formed. The next General Assembly (1849) divided the synod and created a new synod to be known as Brazos Synod, record of which we quote:

"Whereas the territory now embraced in Texas Synod is so extensive as to subject the members thereof to great inconvenience, labor, and expense in attending its meetings. And whereas, there are now six presbyteries reported to the General Assembly within the bounds of said Synod. Therefore,

"Resolved, That the Trinity, Frazier, and Colorado Presbyteries be stricken from said Synod, and be constituted into a new Synod, to be known by the name of Brazos Synod of the Cumberland Presbyterian Church, and that it hold its first meeting in the Town of Huntsville, State of Texas, on Thursday before the first Sabbath in November next; and that Rev. F. E. Foster be the first Moderator of the Synod, or in case of his absence, Rev. Milton Estill."

The records show that Rev. R. Waters represented Frazier Presbytery in the General Assembly of 1850. The only directory of Frazier Presbytery appearing in the General Assembly Minutes, that of 1854, shows the ministers of that presbytery to be J. S. Guthric, Woodville Priest, A. J. McGown, and Milton Estill. This presbytery, which comprised a portion of southeastern Texas centering around Huntsville, was shortlived, being dissolved in 1857. Another presbytery was organized in that part of the state a few years later which was known for many years as San Jacinto Presbytery.

Marshall Presbytery embraced the territory between the Sabine and Sulphur Fork. Rev. G. S. Templeton represented this presbytery in the General Assembly of 1849. Other ministers who labored in this presbytery during the earlier years of its existence included the Revs. Solomon Awalt and T. B. Wilson, concerning whose labors we have already spoken, L. T. Hudiburgh, S. R. Chadick, and John Overton Parr.

Rev. L. T. Hudiburgh was the organizer of the Daingerfield church which was organized on March 11, 1849, with twenty-nine members. The elders were Patrick Martin and William Norwood. Chapel Hill College was soon afterward established there, which brought some strong preachers to that church, and under the ministry of such men as Revs. J. A. Zinn, S. R. Chadick, W. E. Beeson, and W. M. Allen the church grew rapidly and flourished for many years.

Rev. S. R. Chadick came to Texas in the fall of 1850, and with his father-in-law, Jacob Fisher, settled in the Pine Tree community. That year he taught school at "Paradise Lost," near Jefferson, and preached at Jefferson, holding services in the Methodist Protestant church in the village on Sunday morning and at his schoolhouse in the afternoon. Two years later, after he had moved to Daingerfield and was preaching and teaching there, he organized the Cumberland Presbyterian church in Jefferson with six members. The distance of thirty miles from Daingerfield to his appointment at Jefferson he would travel on horseback, preaching Sunday morning and afternoon and riding home Sunday night so as to be in the school room Monday morning. After five and a half years spent in teaching and preaching at Daingerfield, he established an academy at Coffeeville, Upshur County, where he also took charge of the small Cumberland Presbyterian congregation and established a camp ground where meetings were held for a number of years. In later years he again served the Daingerfield church as pastor and at the age of seventy-five rode the distance of thirty miles on horseback from his home at Gilmer to fill his monthly appointments at Daingerfield.

Rev. John Overton Parr came to the vicinity or Marshall in the fall of 1849. He had entered the ministry in Missouri several years before, but was not ordained until after he came to Texas. As he had grown up on the frontier, his opportunities for obtaining an education were limited, and, like many other preachers in that day, he had to work hard for a living, as he got little or no financial support from the churches. He was in the truck and dairy business near Marshall, and many times when his work was crowding him so that he could not leave home on Saturdays he would get up before day on Sunday morning, split a pine torch and carry with him to give him light through the forest until day, then ride eighteen or twenty miles by eleven o'clock, preach again that night, and after the night service return home to be at his work on Monday.

He devoted himself principally to missionary work in the waste places, preaching at schoolhouses where the people were destitute of the preached Word. It is said that the largest salary he ever received was one hundred dollars per year for one-fourth time, and that was at Elysian Fields, near the Louisiana and Texas line, where there was one lone Cumberland Presbyterian family who got him to come there and preach. It was a Methodist community, but they never let him quit preaching to them until he left that part of the country. Another place he built up a good congregation and arrangements for calling another and better educated preacher were being considered. The sinners of the community said, "No, he has got to preach for us, and we will pay him ourselves," and they did. He lived at Marshall until 1857 when he moved west to Grayson County. During the war he moved to Daingerfield to send his children to school and died there in 1868.

The six sons of John Overton Parr all became elders in the Cumberland Presbyterian Church. The eldest, Joe C. Parr, was made an elder in the Daingerfield church in 1870, and at the next meeting of presbytery was elected a member of the board of directors of Chapel Hill College, then under the care of Marshall Presbytery. He died February 11, 1936, at Denton, at the age of ninety-one years, sixty-six of which was spent as a ruling elder in the Cumberland Presbyterian Church. Other members of this Parr family are and have been for many years prominently connected with the church in Northwest Texas. Osborn Parr and B. T. Parr (better known as "Uncle Berry") were long time elders in the Diamound church, in Montague County. Zeno H. Parr was for many years an elder in the church at Justin, Denton County. These were brothers of John Overton Parr.*

## BEGINNING OF THE CHURCH IN KAUFMAN COUNTY

In the spring of 1854 Rev. R. O. Watkins received a letter from some members of his church at Nacogdoches who had moved to Kaufman County, stating that they had no one to break the bread of life to them and asking that a minister be sent. Upon investigating as to the bounds of the several new pres-

*According to M. J. Parr, Dallas, Texas.

byteries that had been created, he found that this territory was not included in any of the new presbyteries and was, therefore, still a part of Texas Presbytery, of which Watkins was a member. Accordingly, in May of that year he visited Kaufman County, spent several weeks preaching in different parts of the county and hunting up the Cumberland Presbyterians, and set a time for all of them to meet him at the county seat, at which time he organized a Cumberland Presbyterian church **embracing the whole county.** Before returning home he made appointments for two camp meetings to be held in different parts of the county that fall.

In September he again set out for Kaufman County, this time accompanied by Rev. S. W. McCorkle, a young minister who had recently been ordained. Both meetings were successful, and arrangements were made for McCorkle to move on the field immediately. The following year Watkins himself moved to Kaufman County, making his home at Kemp.

A number of strong churches were established in Kaufman County which was soon included in White Rock Presbytery and afterward became a part of Bacon Presbytery at its organization. At the present time, however, the only active Cumberland Presbyterian church in the county is Camp Ground, north of Terrell, which is under the care of Dallas Presbytery.

## NEW PRESBYTERIES

White Rock Presbytery was formed by Texas Synod in the fall of 1854, and comprised a large territory to the north and east of Dallas.

Greenville Presbytery was formed in 1855. Not

much data is at hand regarding early ministers and churches in that presbytery. Rev. S. R. Chadick, in an autobiographical sketch, mentions having attended a camp meeting near Mt. Vernon in 1851 where he met with the committee which employed him to take charge of the school which was then being established at Daingerfield. The Mt. Zion church, near Commerce, has a history dating back to 1849. This congregation, originally called Harmony, was organized by Rev. Anthony Travelstead with thirteen members, the elders being David Findley, John Rucker, and F. Marrs. Under the ministry of the twenty or more pastors who have served this church, it has continued through the years a vital factor in the religious life of the community. Many of its members have gone out from this community and helped to establish and carry on the church in other localities.

Bacon presbytery, named for the pioneer Cumberland Presbyterian preacher of Texas, was formed in 1856. This presbytery embraced the counties of Kaufman, Van Zandt, Henderson, and Smith.

### SHILOH (ELLIS COUNTY)

The oldest church of any Protestant denomination west of the Trinity River and north of the old San Antonio Road is the Shiloh Cumberland Presbyterian Church, located in Ellis County.

Rev. Finis E. King, who was the potent factor in the organization of this church, came to Texas from Missouri in the year 1846. He was a son of Rev. Samuel King, one of the founders of the Cumberland Presbyterian Church. At the time of his coming to Texas he was a licentiate under the care of Lexington

Presbytery. As he was not yet ordained, and hence not authorized to organize churches, he sent to Paris, Texas, for Rev. J. C. Provine, who came and officiated in the organization of the Shiloh church on July 5, 1847. The petition of that date setting forth the fact of the organization follows:

"We, the undersigned, inhabitants of the counties of Navarro and Dallas in the State of Texas, having been members of the Cumberland Presbyterian Church previous to our removal to this country, and being willing to support the gospel of Christ our Savior, and have it preached, and the ordinances of God's house administered unto us, agree to form ourselves into a congregation under the care of the Cumberland Presbyterian Church, and submit to the Government thereof, and look to her for such supplies of the means of grace as she may from time to time afford to us."

This petition is signed by F. E. King (minister), Sarah King, James E. Patton (elder), Mary E. Patton, E. C. Newton, Sarah Newton, Martha Billingsley, Katherine Kimble, Eliza Mitchel, Mary Wallace, James Billingsley (elder), Mary Newton, Wm. C. Billingsley, Susan J. Billingsley, Pollard Kirkland, Margarette Kirkland, Arrena Kirkland, Sarah Garvin, John S. Patton, and Jane Laughlin. These had come to this part of Texas during 1845 and 1846. As will be seen from the above, the organization of the Shiloh church took place before Ellis County was formed.

In the above petition it will be noted that the name of the presbytery in which the congregation was located is omitted, the reason being that this congregation was isolated and so far away from a presbytery that it was not known at the time in what bounds they lived. Up until this time, however, no other presby-

SHILOH CHURCH, ELLIS COUNTY, TEXAS

REV. F. E. KING'S GRAVE
in the Shiloh cemetery

teries except Colorado had been formed west of the Trinity, so we find that Rev. F. E. King attended the fall meeting of Colorado Presbytery in 1847 at Gonzales, Texas, and, on petition of the Shiloh church, was ordained to the full work of the gospel ministry.

In a Memorial and Biographical History of Ellis County, published in 1892, it is said of Rev. F. E. King, "He has justly been called the pioneer of Ellis County, in religious matters."

He was pastor of the Shiloh church from its organization until his death, which occurred in September, 1859. Under his ministry the membership of tne Shiloh church was built up to approximately 250. He also organized a number of other congregations in Ellis and adjoining counties, thus laying the foundation for Red Oak Presbytery, which was formed by the Brazos Synod in 1855 and was for many years a stronghold of Cumberland Presbyterianism in Texas, having in its membership some of the ablest ministers in the state. Rev. F. E. King attended the General Assembly in 1858 as the first commissioner from this presbytery.

After his death, an older brother, Rev. R. D. King, who had removed from Missouri to the Shiloh neighborhood, served the church as pastor for six months. He had traveled extensively as a pioneer preacher in several states, having had much to do with planting the Cumberland Presbyterian Church in Alabama, Arkansas, and Missouri. He was a man of strong determination, which quality no doubt had much to do with carrying him through and making it possible for him successfully to combat sickness, swim swollen streams, and endure perils innumerable in order to meet his appointments. He spent the remainder of his life in Texas, and passed to his reward from his home in Hamilton County in 1882.

The next pastor of the Shiloh church was Rev. C. W. Berry, who also was from Missouri. He was followed by Rev. Daniel G. Molloy, a native of Indiana, who was educated at Canehill (Arkansas) College and who was pastor of the Shiloh church from 1861 to 1880, during which time a membership of from 250 to 300 was maintained. He was followed by Rev. Samuel Richards, D.D., from Illinois, and formerly a professor in Lincoln University. Other pastors who have served this church include Revs. B. M. White, James Williams, James Martiens, W. M. Bunch, Clay Collier, N. H. Patterson, Henry Baker, O. N. Baucom, G. L. Waddle, E. R. Duggins, J. L. Elliott, and A. H. Bates (present pastor).

Of the elders of this church we would mention one or two particularly. E. C. Newton, one of the charter members and for nearly fifty years clerk of the session, lived until 1898. He had a long career of usefulness in church and state. It is related that when a little boy the first money he ever earned he paid for a Bible, and throughout his long and eventful life that book was his companion. He married the widow of Rev. F. E. King.

J. W. Bryson came to this community before the Civil War, and shortly after his return from that conflict joined the church with his wife, who had been converted during the war, and was soon afterward made a ruling elder. He was the grandfather of Rev. Davis O. Bryson, also a product of this church, who

is now at home on furlough after four years' missionary service in Colombia, South America.

During the first forty-four years of this church's
history, under the pastorate of nine ministers, thousands were converted, and fifteen hundred had united
with the Shiloh church. Many of these went to other
portions of the country and formed the nuclei of other
congregations.

Although there are now four other churches in the
community, Shiloh continues in the front line, having
a membership of more than a hundred, and is a very
vital force in the religious life of the community.

## EARLY HISTORY OF TEHUACANA*

Major John Boyd, a native of Tennessee who came
to Texas in the fall of 1835 and immediately cast his
lot with the Texas army, received for his services a
"league and labor" of land,** which he located on a
range of hills called Tehuacana Hills (originally spelled
Tywacana), so named after a tribe of Indians, the first
known inhabitants of this section of the state. The
land which he received was at that time in Robertson
County, but was afterward cut off into a new county

---

*From MS. history of Tehuacana, by Rev. J. W. Pearson, and
obituary of Rev. R. E. Sanders, by Rev. J. S. Groves, in *The Cumberland Presbyterian*, Vol. 53, p. 511.

**When Stephen F. Austin went to Mexico and applied for a
section of land (640 acres) for each family in his colony, the Mexican officers misunderstood the term "section" and supposed he
meant township. They replied that that was too much land for a
single family, but they were willing to give each one a league (4,428
acres) for grazing purposes, and an additional "labor" (177 acres)
for cultivation.—Thrall.

known as Limestone. Major Boyd moved on his land in 1845 and settled at the Boyd Spring, near what is now known as Barry Springs. At that time the nearest settlement was old Fort Parken near old Springfield on the Navasota River. Major Boyd took an active part in state and county affairs, and when the time came for Texas to select a site for a state capital, he placed Tehuacana as a candidate for the place, and rode from settlement to settlement advocating and pointing out the advantages of Tehuacana Hills as a suitable place for the state capital. Austin, as we know, won the contest, which is said to have been very close.

Reuben E. Sanders, the pioneer preacher in the Tehuacana region, was born in Cooper County, Missouri, March 17, 1822, professed religion at the age of six years, and joined the church at the age of seven. He was received under the care of Lexington Presbytery in 1844 and was licensed in 1846. He came to Texas early in the year 1848 and joined Colorado Presbytery, by which presbytery he was soon afterward ordained.

Major Boyd at that time was not a Christian, though he had the highest respect for Christianity and sought every opportunity to aid any minister of the gospel who might be passing that way. He induced Reuben Sanders to locate on his league of land. He also advocated and aided in building a log schoolhouse. Here, under the leadership of Reuben Sanders, the residents from far and wide gathered to worship, coming on horseback and in ox wagons, bringing their guns with them and stacking them in the chimney corner, one man being appointed as a picket to watch for the Indians while services were held.

Reuben Sanders labored in this region for many years, enduring the hardships of the frontier and riding horseback hundreds of miles each month to preach the gospel of Christ to the scattered settlers. Frequently he had to swim swollen streams to reach his appointments, or slept out in the open with his saddle for a pillow while the wolves made the night hideous with their howling. Though the distances were great, he rarely ever missed a meeting of presbytery or synod. On one occasion he and one of his elders were en route to the meeting of Colorado Presbytery at Austin, when they put up at a certain house to spend the night. The next morning they asked their host the bill for the night's lodging. He replied that the elder was a farmer and stock raiser and worked hard for a living and there would be no charge for him, but as the preacher did not work and made a living easy, he would charge him a dollar and a quarter. Sanders pulled out his purse and paid the bill, which took all the money he had with him. He had received for his ministerial services during the year just closing the sum of five dollars. This was an unusual case, as almost every family in that day was glad to entertain the preacher who might be passing that way. Sanders is described as a man of one book, that book being his Bible. He was a slow and deliberate, but earnest, speaker. He entered into rest November 20, 1894 after a ministry of fifty years.

In the early days of his ministry at Tehuacana, Reuben Sanders invited Rev. Andrew J. McGown to hold a camp meeting near the old schoolhouse. As

Major Boyd and McGown both were soldiers, the Major was at once attracted to him. Soon after the meeting began, one night when McGown had made one of his famous appeals for penitents to come to the mourner's bench, Major Boyd responded and came and knelt in the altar along with a number of others. While some were crying aloud for mercy and others shouting over their new-found joy, and Sanders and McGown were moving among them giving instruction and comfort, McGown came near where Major Boyd had been kneeling and found he had got up from the mourner's bench and was sitting in a chair clapping his hands. "What's the matter with you, Major Boyd?" McGown asked.

"The Lord has converted my soul," replied the Major, "for which I want the water poured on my head."

Near by was a pitcher of water, so McGown reached for pitcher, raised it above the major's head and said, "Major Boyd, I baptize you in the name of the Father, and the Son, and the Holy Ghost," and then and there poured the water on his head. Notwithstanding the shouting mingled with mourning in the altar, there was no confusion, and all this was done "in decency and in order." This incident was witnessed by Samuel B. Campbell, son-in-law of the Major, and told to Rev. J. W. Pearson in later years by him. After this, Major Boyd joined the Cumberland Presbyterian Church under the ministry of Rev. Reuben Sanders.

Tehuacana Hills constituted a well known landmark in the early days of Texas. From their heights the eye takes in a radius of twenty to twenty-five miles of surrounding prairie.

Tehuacana Presbytery was formed in 1851 or 1852,

being the second presbytery organized west of the Trinity River.

## HISTORY OF THE CORSICANA CHURCH

The first record of the Corsicana congregation is the petition of twenty Cumberland Presbyterians to be taken under the care of Tehuacana Presbytery. The charter members of this church, which was organized May 16, 1853, were R. N. White, James Kerr, Sr., and Nancy Kerr, James R. Campbell and Lucy A. Campbell, Thomas Jackson and Elizabeth Jackson, Nancy Byers, Jeremiah Cunningham and Polly Cunningham, Caroline Goade, Emmaline Lindsey, E. R. Story and Margaret E. Story, E. C. Story and Martha J. Story, and servant girl, Savanna, S. H. Kerr and Mrs. C. D. Kerr, and Mrs. Margaret Riggs. The Corsicana congregation was organized by Rev. John S. Patton, T. N. McKey, and Jeremiah Cunningham.

In the early days of the church, on account of small membership, it was impossible to get a regular pastor, but the congregation had Sunday school regularly, and preaching once a month by such men as Revs. J. S. Patton, R. D. King, R. B. and John S. Groves, Jeremiah Cunningham, and Griggsby until 1857, when Rev. N. P. Modrall was employed as pastor. He served ten years, and was followed by Rev. Willis Burgess and Rev. Alpha Young, each of whom served four years.

The first church building, which was erected soon after the organization, was located in the 700 block between Second and Third Avenues. It was the only church building in the town until the Methodists built a church on their present location, and the Cumberlands opened their house to any Protestant denomination which wished to use it. Under the ministry of Rev. Alpha Young, a brick church was built on the lot now occupied by the Third Avenue Presbyterian Church. This was completed and dedicated in 1874. Among the pastors who served the congregation while it was worshiping in this building were Revs. T. M. Goodknight, A. Templeton, W. G. Templeton, E. B. Crisman, W. S. Danley, and J. A. Ward.

In 1884 a Second Cumberland Presbyterian Church was erected in East Corsicana, which was served by Revs. W. J. Lackey and J. W. Hornbeak, but after about three years, the venture not proving a success, this Second Church building was sold and the proceeds used to build the first manse owned by the Corsicana congregation. A new church building was erected under the ministry of Rev. J. A. Ward and completed in 1891, and was used until 1906 when, of a membership of 386, 180 refused to go into the proposed union with the Presbyterian Church, U.S.A., and those who chose to remain in the Cumberland Presbyterian Church were enjoined by the union element from holding services in this church. In June, 1906, it was decided to go to the Carnegie Hall, where the organization was continued under the leadership of Rev. W. J. Lackey as pastor. In 1908 the Corsicana congregation was host to the Eighty-Eighth General Assembly. On Sunday, April 11, 1915, the present building, located on Twelfth Street, which had been purchased and remodeled, was dedicated by Rev. J. W. Hornbeak, using as a text, "The glory of the Lord filled the house." Among those who have had most to do with perpetuating the Cumberland Presbyterian Church in Corsicana are some of the descendants of the original charter members.

## COLORADO SYNOD

Brazos Synod, at its 1853 meeting, created two new presbyteries out of the territory formerly occupied by Colorado Presbytery, namely, Guadalupe and Little River. At the same meeting the General Assembly was requested to form a new synod consisting of Little River, Guadalupe, and Colorado Presbyteries. The request was granted and the new synod was called Colorado Synod. According to the order of the General Assembly, the first meeting was held at Bastrop on Thursday before the second Sabbath in November, 1854. Rev. Henry Renick was appointed the first moderator, and Rev. Andrew Herron his alternate.

Little River Presbytery at that time comprised the territory which later became Waco and San Saba Presbyteries, together with Williamson, Burnet, and neighboring counties. Included in its bounds was almost everything west of the Brazos and north of Austin, as far north as Stephenville and west as far as there were people. Because of the connection of quite a few of the older churches of this presbytery with the history of those other presbyteries of which they later became a part, we are reserving the history of this presbytery until a later period.

Among the ministers who appear on the roll of Colorado Presbytery before the Civil War are Revs. A. J. Adkisson, Henry Renick, George Golden, and E. B. Crisman. Rev. E. B. Crisman was located at Austin for a period of four years from 1853 to 1857. Rev. Henry Renick came from McGee Presbytery, Missouri, where he had a ministry reaching back into the eighteen twenties, before the General Assembly was organized. Rev. George Golden was licensed to preach at seventeen years of age near Waynesburg, Pennsylvania, which was his native home. He came to Texas in 1845, then went to Princeton, Kentucky, to school for two years, after which ill health necessitated his return to Texas. He then taught school and preached, first in Colorado Presbytery and later in Guadalupe Presbytery. He was ordained by Colorado Presbytery at Bastrop before the division to form Guadalupe Presbytery. He preached at Lockhart and other places, and in 1874 and 1875 led in the building of a Cumberland Presbyterian Church at Rockdale. He died April 27, 1911, at the age of eighty-six years, being at the time of his death a member of Corsicana-Waco Presbytery.

Revs. A. H. Walker, W. H. Crutcher, and George Golden all figured prominently in the early history of Guadalupe Presbytery. Rev. A. H. Walker had been pastor at LaGrange before 1850, and later preached in the vicinity of Gonzales.

Another minister whose memory is enshrined in the hearts of many was Rev. J. J. A. Roach, who lived and preached at Mountain City, in Hays County, during the period just following the Civil War.

Rev. William Marshall Love, a medical doctor and preacher, came to Texas in 1850, and after spending some time in the vicinity of Marshall, he moved to Washington County where he remained until 1867, during which time he labored in Fayette, Bastrop, Travis, and Washington Counties, with revival and evangelistic work in the surrounding districts. He then moved to Yellow Prairie, now known as Chriesman, where he lived until his death two years later.

By 1857 the Cumberland Presbyterian Church had

three synods comprising a total of twelve presbyteries in the state of Texas, and many of our strongest churches in various sections of the state had been established.

## THE CIVIL WAR PERIOD

With the outbreak of the Civil War, the church in Texas was virtually cut off from the General Assembly which met north of the line of battle each year. The Texas presbyteries had no commissioners present at the General Assembly from the beginning of the war until 1866. In the course of that conflict almost every able-bodied man was drawn into the war. This included most of the preachers who were of military age. Several received appointments as chaplains, among them being Revs. John Hudson, S. R. Chadick, and S. M. Lewis. Others served as privates in the regular ranks. Rev. Samuel Corley, who held the rank of major, was killed in action and was buried in the Confederate cemetery at Helena, Arkansas.

As to the demoralizing effect of war upon the churches back at home, permit us to quote from the autobiography of Rev. R. O. Watkins:

"And now commenced the sad work of disastrous war, churches left without pastors, deprived of their Rulers, throughout the bounds of presbytery. Calls everywhere by the destitute, sad, bereaved and suffering in every way almost for someone to come to them in their sorrow and destitution to break to them the bread of life and give the consolations of the Gospel."

After the war was over, then commenced the task of rebuilding the churches which had been scattered and broken up by the war. Again we quote from Rev. R. O. Watkins' autobiography:

"In the fall after the war closed Texas Synod convened at the Town of Kaufman, attendance small, and most of members present were men enfeebled by age, pressed down with increased cares, mourning the loss of loved ones and sad in view of the ruined conditions of the church. In the transaction of appropriate business of Synod the report from committee on state of religion or condition of the church within the Synodical bounds came up, and sad indeed was the report made. Presbyteries nearly annihilated, churches left without preaching, many in disorganized condition, members sad, discouraged, not knowing what to do or where to go for aid, preachers pecuniarily ruined, pressed down with hard labours to secure even the bread necessary to feed their families."

This synod called for a missionary to travel throughout its bounds to visit the discouraged churches and try to bring preachers and churches together. Rev. R. O. Watkins responded, not because he felt that he was the best man for the work, but because he knew of none whose financial condition was more favorable than his. He was appointed synodical missionary for Texas Synod, and for more than a year traveled throughout the bounds of the synod in this work of rallying the scattered forces of the church and bringing order out of chaos.

Although conditions during the war were such as would seem to make aggressive church work almost an impossibility, not all work was suspended, for we find that two new presbyteries were created during this period: Huntsville, which was created in 1863 as South Trinity Presbytery, and the name changed to Huntsville the following year, which was in the bounds of Brazos Synod, and Guthrie Presbytery, which was created by Texas Synod in 1864. The name of Huntsville Presbytery was changed to San Jacinto in 1870.

## HISTORY OF THE DENTON CHURCH

The Cumberland Presbyterian Church at Denton was organized by Rev. R. R. Dunlap in 1862. Revs. M. B. Donald, John Haynes, and W. R. Baker were pastors until 1874 when Rev. D. R. Grafton became pastor and served nine years. During his pastorate two church houses were built. The first one burned while occupied by the District Court.

During the period from 1886 to 1906 Revs. H. G. Nicholson, R. W. Benge, W. H. Berry, T. J. Richards, D. C. DeWitt, A. B. C. Dinwiddie, F. T. Carlton, J. H. Curry, and F. L. Wear were pastors. Under the ministry of Rev. J. H. Curry a new church was built at a cost of about $8,500.

Under the leadership of Rev. F. L. Wear who was pastor in 1906 a majority of the congregation went into the Presbyterian Church, U.S.A., and remained in possession of the church. From thirty to fifty members remained in the Cumberland Presbyterian Church and were forced to seek a place of worship elsewhere. For some time they held services in the court house at such times as they could secure the services of some one of the few Cumberland ministers who could render assistance, but with no church home and no regular preaching the congregation gradually diminished. In 1925 when Rev. J. L. Elliott moved to Denton in order that his youngest daughter might complete her education, there were less than a dozen of the members of the Denton Cumberland Presbyterian Church to be found. The only two remaining elders were J. C. Parr and W. W. Baxter.

W. W. Baxter passed away the following year, but

J. C. Parr and others continued the name of the Denton church on the presbyterial roll, each year collecting dues from the remaining members and contributing to the various enterprises of the church, until the very few who still remained saw the reorganization of the church and the erection of a splendid church house.

On the evening of September 6, 1932, a number of Cumberland Presbyterians gathered at the orphans' home which had been purchased but was not yet occupied, and with Rev. J. L. Elliott presiding, a reorganization of the Denton church was effected with twenty-one members, including four of the original membership, namely, J. C. Parr, Mrs. J. C. Parr, Mrs. Scripture, and Mrs. Wiley Pockrus. The other members included some who had moved to Denton from other places, and some who were members of the Sunnydale church, a near-by rural congregation, the membership of which was eventually brought into the Denton church. D. J. Burrow and R. S. Dobbins were added to the eldership at the reorganization.

Shortly afterward Rev. J. L. Elliott accepted a call as pastor of the Denton church. Services were continued in the orphans' home for several months until a new brick veneer church building was erected in the residential section of the city. This church has grown to a membership of 71 resident and 11 non-resident members, with a Sunday school of approximately one hundred enrolled, active young people's societies, and the usual missionary organizations. The church is situated conveniently to the Cumberland Presbyterian Orphans' Home which was located at Denton by order of the General Assembly in 1932, and to the North Texas State Teachers' College.

## DALLAS, FIRST CHURCH

The first Cumberland Presbyterian preacher who is known to have preached in Dallas was Rev. Daniel Gideon Malloy, who visited Dallas in 1847 and preached

First Cumberland Presbyterian Church built in Dallas, 1869

in the old log court house. In 1853 he returned, and being unable to find a better place, preached in Monsieur Brousseard's saloon. However, we do not have any record of a church being organized until 1867.

The first Cumberland Presbyterian Church in Dallas was organized in 1867 by Rev. A. J. Haynes. Among the charter members were a Mr. and Mrs. McHorn, Mr. and Mrs. Jeff Williams, a Mr. and Mrs. Baker, Miss Ann Ross, Mrs. Hancock, Mr. and Mrs. B. F. Jones, Mr. and Mrs. Ben Lacy, and a Dr. Stevenson. Rev. A. J. Haynes served as the pastor of this congregation for some two or three years, and in 1869 led in the erection of a church building, the second church of any denomination to be built in Dallas. Among those who belonged to the church when it was worshiping at this location, though not a charter member, was Mrs. Ashley B. Moore (widow of the late Rev. Ashley B. Moore, a Cumberland Presbyterian preacher who recently died at Springfield, Missouri) who is now a member of the Oak Cliff Cumberland Presbyterian Church. Rev. Henry F. Bone succeeded Rev. A. J. Haynes as pastor.

In 1890 Rev. D. G. Malloy organized the Trinity Cumberland Presbyterian Church in Oak Cliff. In the meantime the First Church moved to a location opposite where the city hall and the library are now located. In 1906 the Cumberland Presbyterians lost their title to this property. Deprived of a place to worship, they purchased property on the corner of Main Street and Hill Avenue, moving later to Washington Avenue and Simpson, and from there to their present location on the corner of Beacon Street and Ash Lane.

This in brief is the history of the First Cumberland Presbyterian Church of Dallas. Today there are in Dallas nine churches of the Presbyterian Church U.S.A., eight Presbyterian, U.S., and only two Cumberland Presbyterian; but the First Cumberland Presbyterian Church did the pioneering. Long before other members of the Presbyterian family came, this church was here making people love the Presbyterian family.

\* \* \*

Rev. A. J. Haynes, the organizer of the first Cumberland Presbyterian Church in Dallas, was born in the state of Mississippi, September 22, 1822. When twelve years of age he moved with his parents to Graves County, Kentucky. He professed religion and united with the Cumberland Presbyterian Church in his nineteenth year, and two years afterward was received under the care of Obion Presbytery as a candidate for the ministry. He attended Bethel College, then located at McLemoresville, Tennessee, and two years, 1850-52, was a tutor in that institution. On January 29, 1852, he was united in marriage to Miss Melissa Ann Patterson, daughter of an elder in the church and a trustee of the college.

In 1852 he moved to Arkansas, and in 1859 to Fannin County, Texas. For two years he preached at Honey Grove, Bonham, and Shiloh. In 1861 he was called to take charge of the church at Sherman where he stayed two years, during which time he held a successful revival at Gainesville and organized a church in that city.

He then moved to Ellis County, which was his home for fifteen years. It was he who was chosen to guide the spiritual destiny of what was known as the Tennessee Colony, made up of the McKnight, Crabtree, and Andrews families, who traded their land in Tennessee for a "league and labor" of land between the Trinity River and the fork of Ten Mile Creek in about the year 1850 and moved to Texas. In this colony were several men who had been elders in the Cumberland Presbyterian Church in Tennessee, and a church was organized with I. C. Haynes, B. F. Crabtree, Major John Andrews, and Adolphus and George McKnight as elders, services being held in a schoolhouse known as Antioch. In 1870 this colony was enlarged by a group of settlers from Mississippi, among whom were W. R. Duff, S. R. Green, and R. G. Sanders, who had been elders in a Cumberland Presbyterian church known as New Harmony, in Mississippi. Because of the growth of the congregation, services were then held in the Grange Hall, during which time a meeting of synod was held here. In 1872 the railroad was built through this section and the town of Ferris laid out, and a few years later this congregation erected a church building in the town of Ferris.

He also preached at Mansfield, Chambers Creek, and other places. It was during this period also that he organized the church in Dallas.

Besides organizing many churches, he had much to do with the founding of Trinity University and served as financial agent for that institution for three years. In 1882 he moved west and located at Buffalo Gap where he resumed his missionary work on the frontier and was instrumental in establishing another institution of learning in what was then the far west. He died at Buffalo Gap, December 13, 1897.

## MISSIONARIES AND MISSION STATIONS

In 1844, the next year after the organization of Texas Synod, an appeal was made to the church in the United States for help. Several presbyteries responded to this call. Rev. S. F. Donnell was aided by

Lebanon Presbytery in going to Texas, and Rev. T. N. McKee by Elk Presbytery. Rev. S. F. Donnell located in the Red River section where he labored for several years with much success. He had just been appointed agent for the Board of Missions when his death occurred October 16, 1850. Rev. T. N. McKee located first on the Guadalupe River, but later moved to Larissa, Cherokee County. In 1847 the Board of Missions assisted Revs. Robert Waters and J. C. Matthews in moving to Texas.

In 1853 Rev. E. B. Crisman was sent as a missionary to Austin* where a small houseless congregation awaited him. Only the walls had been erected and the roof constructed. He spent four years there, during which time a large membership was gathered and the house of worship completed and paid for. This work, which was interrupted by the war, was resumed in 1866 under the leadership of Rev. Finis E. Foster, to whose support the Board of Missions contributed one hundred dollars a year. In 1868 a gracious revival was reported, in which thirty converts had been added to the church, bringing the total additions during the year to around forty members. In 1870 this church was declared self-sustaining.

During the eighteen fifties when Jefferson became a commercial center and steamboats came up the Cypress, Marshall Presbytery made Jefferson a mission station and contributed some two or three hundred dollars per year to the support of this work. The missionary was Rev. Aaron Griggsby, under whose

*Some authorities state that Rev. E. B. Crisman organized the Austin church.

leadership the church soon grew to be self-sustaining. This work was interrupted with the outbreak of the war. During the troublesome days following the close of the war, however, the work was revived under the leadership of Rev. S. R. Chadick. He was succeeded by Rev. N. P. Modrall, D.D., under whose pastorate the brick church was built. This church was host to the General Assembly in 1875.

Houston and Galveston were frequently mentioned during this period as prospective mission points. In 1851 the missionary society of Frazier Presbytery was reported to be collecting funds to be appropriated toward establishing a mission in Galveston, but so far as the records show this work never materialized. Nothing was done toward establishing a church in Houston until a much later date.

### EARLY SCHOOLS AND COLLEGES

Cumberland Presbyterian preachers were among the first school teachers in Texas. We have already noted the fact that Sumner Bacon taught school in San Augustine County in 1831. The first presbytery resolved to establish a "seminary of learning."

In 1850 Rev. and Mrs. Weyman L. Adair came to Texas and located in the village of Cincinnati, on the south bank of the Trinity River in Walker County, twelve miles north of Huntsville. The Rev. Mr. Adair, a graduate of Cumberland University, Lebanon, Tennessee, conducted the Cincinnati boarding school for three years until 1853, when a stranger came to the village who was very ill. There being no one in the hotel willing to nurse him, Rev. Adair volunteered and took care of him until he died, after which it was learned that he had the dreaded yellow fever. Adair became ill with the yellow fever and died, and the whole village was wiped out by the scourge.

Sometime prior to the Civil War, Rev. John Collier established a school on the Bosque River near Bosqueville, known as Bosque Academy, which did a great work in its day. Among the young preachers who were educated here was Rev. R. B. Davis, who became one of the greatest preachers Little River Presbytery ever had. The old stone building on the banks of the Bosque River is said to be still standing, a lone monument to the memory of its founder and the young preacher sent out from its wall.

A number of schools were established by Cumberland Presbyterians prior to the Civil War. It is difficult to tell in every case whether they were sponsored by the church as such. There were, however, three schools under the care of the Cumberland Presbyterian Church which attained to the rank of colleges: Larissa College, LaGrange Collegiate Institute (later known as Ewing College), and Chapel Hill College.

## LARISSA COLLEGE

From the General Assembly minutes of 1848 the following excerpt is taken:

"A Presbyterial School under the care of the Trinity Presbytery, in Texas, has been lately established, and is in quite flourishing condition. Arrangements have been made for a Presbyterial School at LaGrange, Texas, which is to be under the patronage of the Colorado Presbytery, and to go into operation next fall."

Larissa College was founded in 1848 in a little log hut on the outskirts of the village of the same name which was located in Cherokee County, about three miles west of where the village of Mt. Selman now stands. Thomas H. McKee and Nathaniel Killough each gave a thousand dollars toward founding the enterprise. Mrs. S. R. Erwin, a woman educated in Lebanon, Tennessee, was its first teacher. Rev. T. N. McKee took charge upon her retirement. In the year 1855 this institution was incorporated and chartered as a college under the direction of the Brazos Synod. The first board of trustees, as announced in the catalogue of 1856-57, consisted of Nathaniel Killough (president), S. R. McGowan (secretary), S. A. Erwin (treasurer), Thomas Smith, William B. Campbell, S. W. Erwin, Bush Wofford, Thomas McKee, Y. D. Harrington, Rev. T. N. McKee, W. A. Dunning, R. K. Gaston, and James D. Long. During this session there were 144 students enrolled, including three candidates for the ministry.

In 1857-58 there was a decline in students, the female department being suspended. The school struggled for existence, and it was thought that it had reached a crisis.

When the Brazos Synod met in 1859 the tide of interest was rising again. The female department had been revived and the attendance was good. Rev. F. L. Yoakum had been elected president for a term of four years; Mrs. H. D. Donald, assistant teacher for one year; and Rev. D. S. Crawford, teacher, in the female department.

During 1859-60 a large telescope, made to order in the principal factory in the United States under the management of Dr. Henry Fitz of New York at a cost of $700, was brought to the school. A splendid set of chemical, philosophical, mathematical, and meteorological instruments had also been procured, and members of the faculty, during their leisure time, had built up quite a collection of geological and minerological specimens. In 1860 Larissa's first and only graduating class of four members was awarded diplomas.

Then came the period of the war,· which forced the suspension of the college. After four years of war the friends of the college revived it and began work again. In 1866 Brazos Synod withdrew its relations from Larissa College. Reduced to a private school, its work was continued under adverse conditions until 1869, when Trinity University was opened, and the property of Larissa College was disposed of and the proceeds turned over to Trinity University.*

## EWING COLLEGE

This institution, located at La Grange, had its beginning under the name of La Grange Collegiate Institute in the fall of 1848. From a diploma issued by this institution March 4, 1850, this information has been gathered: M. A. Montrose was president of the institution, and Elizabeth Montrose, principal. Trustees were W. L. Adkisson, I. B. McFarland, W. B. McClellan, W. F. Hodge, and B. Townsend. This institution was under the control of Colorado Presbytery.

With the organization of Colorado Synod in 1854, the control of the school was transferred to the synod, and its name changed to Ewing College. "In 1855, Prof. R. P. Decherd became president, and the school flourished under his management, and promised to be-

---

*Condensed from data furnished by Mrs. J. B. Brock, Mt. Selman, Texas.

come a permanent institution. Its work was stopped by the breaking out of the war."*

## CHAPEL HILL COLLEGE

The establishment of this institution was sponsored by the Marshall Presbytery. On January 8, 1849, Allen Urkhart gave land for the college on condition that it be built at Daingerfield. The proposition was accepted. The school was opened on the first Monday in February, 1852, in an unfinished wooden building with Rev. S. R. Chadick as teacher. In September following, he was joined by Rev. W. E. Beeson, a former classmate in Cumberland University, who became president of the school. Rev. S. T. Anderson was soon afterward elected professor of mathematics. Rev. W. E. Beeson continued as president of this school until 1869, when he resigned to become president of Trinity University.

In 1852 Chapel Hill College was taken under the care of Texas Synod. During this period many who later became the leading ministers of the Cumberland Presbyterian Church in Texas attended school here, among them, Revs. Benjamin Spencer, J. S. Patton, J. A. Ward, W. S. Glass, S. E. Black, J. C. Blanton, W. Burgess Modrall, C. C. Givens, S. M. Johnston, T. W. Sego, Jerre Shetter, A. W. Johnston, and Y. H. Hamilton.

When Trinity University was established by the three synods in Texas acting jointly, Texas Synod gave its support to that institution and Chapel Hill College reverted back to the Marshall Presbytery. In the

*McDonnold, *History of the Cumberland Presbyterian Church*, p.554.

summer of 1870 Rev. W. M. Allen was elected president
and conducted the school a year. He was a native of
Huntsville, Alabama, where he was born January 18,
1819. He grew up as an orphan boy with practically
no school privileges. It is said of him that he never
attended school but eleven months in his life. After
he entered the ministry in 1842 in Mississippi, he began traveling with other preachers, assisting them in
their work and studying the course prescribed for ordination. He soon became a fine English scholar, after
which he studied Greek, mathematics, philosophy, Hebrew, and literature, carrying textbook in his saddle-
bags as he went from appointment to appointment.
He came to Texas in 1859, and united with Marshall
Presbytery the following year, and was a member of
this presbytery until his death which occurred at Marshall, May 19, 1899. Among the ministerial students
who attended Chapel Hill College under his administration were Revs. S. H. Braly, J. M. Burrow, and W.
B. Allen.

With the institution of the free school laws just
then beginning to become effective, Chapel Hill College
soon had to close its doors, and the buildings were
finally condemned and torn down.

# Chapter III

## TRINITY UNIVERSITY ESTABLISHED—EXPANSION WESTWARD

### (1869-1888)

THE proposal to establish one central educational institution of high order for the church in Texas, which led to the founding of Trinity University,* is generally understood to have originated in a conversation between Rev. A. J. Haynes and Rev. H. F. Bone at Corsicana, Texas, where the latter was teaching, just after the close of the Civil War. This policy had had its advocates at an earlier date, but concerted action had been impossible to secure, due to the fact that the various synodical schools were then in a flourishing condition. Now they had either been wiped out of existence or were badly crippled, and there was the need of doing something to take care of the educational needs of our church in Texas. Be it said, moreover, to the credit of those who had been connected with the older schools, that Trinity University had none who were more loyal in her support than were those whose interests had formerly been centered in the older institutions.

In 1866 the three synods of Brazos, Colorado, and Texas elected delegates to an educational convention, which was held in Dallas the following year, to take under advisement the establishment of a college for the

---

*Sources: Historical sketch of Trinity University by Rev. J. V. Stevens, D.D., in *The Cumberland Presbyterian*, Vol. 60, p. 777; article by D. S. Bodenhamer, in *The Cumberland Presbyterian*, Vol. 53, p. 756; MS. history of Tehuacana, by Rev. J. W. Pearson Individual aid: Judge F. H. Prendergast.

entire church in Texas. The result of this convention
was a recommendation to the three synods that immediate steps be taken to secure bids for the location of
such an institution. Accordingly, in 1868, a joint committee was named to select the location and proceed at
once to establish the school. Bids were received from
Dallas, Round Rock, Waxahachie, and Tehuacana. Major
John Boyd, of Tehuacana, offered to donate to the institution a town site of one hundred and thirty acres on
Tehuacana Hills and fifteen hundred acres of land on
the prairie below, to secure the location of the college
at Tehuacana. After mature and prayerful delibera-
tion, the committee took its final action in a meeting
held at Waco on April 26, 1869, and voted unanimously
to accept Major Boyd's offer of real estate and locate
the school at Tehuacana Hills, Limestone County. Trinity University was the name chosen for this institution,
and arrangements were made to procure a charter, elect
trustees, and have everything in readiness to open the
school that fall. The plan was to sell the land in the
valley, together with the lots in the town site, except
seventeen acres on the hill which was reserved for the
future needs of the school, and use the money in the
erection of buildings.

## TRUSTEES OF TRINITY UNIVERSITY

The original charter provided that there should be
nine trustees, three elected by each of the three synods,
all of whom must live within twelve miles of the college. An amendment to the charter in 1877 provided
that the number of trustees from each synod be increased to four, except that Brazos Synod was to elect

five trustees, and that a majority of the trustees must reside within twelve miles of the institution. With the organization of a fourth synod in 1881, the number of trustees was increased to seventeen.

Among those who composed the original board were some of the outstanding men of that part of Texas.

Dr. J. S. Wills, who moved from Tennessee to Freestone County, Texas, in 1848, and was a ruling elder in the church at Cotton Gin, was chosen as the first president of the board, in which capacity he served until his death, which occurred August 6, 1877.

L. B. Prendergast, second president of the board, was born in what is now Giles County, Tennessee, November 25, 1808. His mother was a sister of Rev. Samuel King, one of the founders of the Cumberland Presbyterian Church. He moved to Texas in 1839 and for some thirty years was a ruling elder and clerk of the session of the old Oak Island church, four miles east of Mexia, which congregation was later moved to Cotton Gin. He was the father of Judge F. H. Prendergast, now of Marshall, Texas. He served as president of the board from the death of Dr. Wills, in 1877, until his own death, March 23, 1885.

His brother, D. M. Prendergast, who succeeded him as president of the board, was born in Shelby County, Tennessee, December 26, 1816, and came to Texas in 1841. He lived to a ripe old age and filled many positions of trust, but none so long as that of a trustee of Trinity University. His heart and soul were in the college, and he gave freely of his time and money to its upbuilding. He served as a trustee and president of the board until 1900. He obtained the charter for Trinity University which was approved August 13, 1870. He also obtained the enactment of a special law on August 15, 1870, which is as follows:

"An act to prohibit the sale of spirituous liquors and the establishing or keeping of any gambling table or device within two miles of 'Trinity University,' in Limestone County.

"Section 1. Be it enacted by the Legislature of the State of Texas, That it shall be unlawful for any person or persons, either with or without license, to sell or offer for sale, or otherwise dispose of, except for medical purposes, any spiritous, vinous, malt or other intoxicating liquors, or establish or keep a ten pin alley, billiard table, or other sporting or gambling table, game, or device within two miles of 'Trinity University,' situated at Tehuacana Hills, Limestone County, Texas; and any one violating the provisions of this section shall be deemed guilty of a misdemeanor, and on conviction thereof before any court of competent jurisdiction, shall be fined in any sum not less than ten or more than one hundred dollars for each and every offense."[*]

This was a very wise provision and serves to illustrate the high sense of morals with which the trustees endeavored to surround the school. Presumably, the provision of this law were abrogated when the university was moved from Tehuacana to Waxahachie.

John Karvin was born in Bavaria on August 15, 1815, and came to America in 1831 and to Texas in 1835. He was a veteran of San Jacinto and of conflicts with the Indians in the early days. He was a man of his word, and supported the board in all of its difficult tasks of building up the school. He was an elder in the Cumberland Presbyterian Church in Tehuacana.

J. H. Bell was born in Guilford County, North Caro-

*Special Laws of Texas, p. 323.

lina, July 14, 1820. He came to Texas in 1859 and settled in Navarro County. In 1863 he joined the Cumberland Presbyterian Church, was elected a member of the board of trustees of Trinity at its organization, and served nine years.

T. W. Wade was made a member of the board of trustees before he joined the Cumberland Presbyterian Church. He was born in Logan County, Kentucky, January 3, 1833, and came to Texas when a small boy. He grew to manhood at old Chatfield, in Navarro County. In 1872 he moved to Tehuacana where he engaged in a general merchandising business with his father and brother. Captain Wade was elected treasurer of the board. There was no vault in which to keep the records and valuable papers safe from fire, so for many years Captain Wade kept all the endowment notes and valuable papers in a small hand grip which never left his sight during the day, and at night it was under his bed, to be the first thing cared for in case of fire. At one time there were thirty-three thousand dollars worth of vendor lien notes and mortgages in that hand grip.

## THE BUILDING PERIOD

In 1869 some friends of the school bought fourteen hundred and twenty acres of land northeast of where the main building was afterward erected, on which was a two story residence with eight large rooms. This residence and fifty acres of land were donated to the school. In this building the school was opened under the presidency of Rev. William E. Beeson, D.D., with an enrollment of two pupils on the first day of school. It looked as if after all the church in Texas cared little for the school; but in a few days students began to arrive, and soon it became apparent that a new building must be provided.

TRINITY UNIVERSITY IN 1869

In 1871 the erection of the administration building on the hill was begun with Rev. Alpha Young as superintendent of the building. The foundation was laid off in the shape of a capital "T" (for Tehuacana and Trinity). The bar of the "T" was built first and was of two stories, with the chapel on the second floor. It was planned to build the two wings to the building later.

In September, 1873, the school opened in the new stone building, leaving the old frame building vacant. This move created some friction between the citizens who lived near the frame building and those who lived on top of the hill. The branch that runs between the two buildings was called the Nile River, and the territory around the old wooden building was dubbed Egypt, and that around the stone building, Africa.

Those who lived across the branch from the stone building would say, "Yes, you have moved to Africa, but you have to come back to Egypt for your bread." There were no boarding houses at that time near the new building, and boarding students had to continue boarding in the homes near the old building, which gave rise to the above saying.

For a number of years the school built up rapidly. The first graduating class consisted of two members: J. L. Modrall and J. Sanford Groves. The former died in 1875 after a brief ministerial career. The latter held several successful pastorates, among them one at Mexia for a period of eighteen years.

Dr. Beeson continued as president, with the exception of one year, until his death which occurred near Hillsboro, Texas, September 5, 1882. He is described as a man of fine sense and excellent education. He was born October 21, 1822, in Berkley County, Virginia. He graduated from Cumberland University in 1849, and while teaching in Bowling Green, Kentucky, in 1852, he was called to the presidency of Chapel Hill College which had just been established at Daingerfield, Texas. From there he was called to be the first president of Trinity University.

From the beginning there were a number of ministerial students enrolled, and as time went on the number increased, although, after about 1880, the total enrollment in all departments began to fall off, due to the number of colleges which were being established in different parts of the state, and, the building up of the public free school system. In 1877 a theological department was established with Dr. Beeson as teacher, and it was during this year that Dr. Beeson retired temporarily from the presidency and R. W. Pittman was acting president for one year. The following year Dr. Beeson resumed the presidency, though continuing as teacher of theology until his death. The report for 1874 shows that there were 16 ministerial students enrolled; in 1881, the number had increased to 20; and in 1888, there were 31. Many of our leading preachers in Texas during the last sixty years were educated at Trinity University.

A law department was also maintained for a time, with D. M. Prendergast, and later R. C. Ewing, as teacher.

Among the teachers who served under the presidency of Dr. Beeson and enjoyed the distinction of long terms of service in connection with the school were W. P. Gillespie, who served from the beginning until 1877 as professor of Latin and Greek, and who, after an absence of a few years resumed his work in this department; Prof. R. P. Decherd, former president of Ewing College at LaGrange, who was professor of mathematics, 1871-77; Rev. S. T. Anderson, D.D., who had been connected with the school at Daingerfield and succeeded Prof. Decherd in the chair of mathematics, remaining here until 1885; Miss Sallie R. Young, daughter of Rev. Alpha Young, who conducted the primary department from 1872 to 1886; and Mrs. M. F. Foster, who taught in the preparatory department, 1872-84.

Following the death of Dr. Beeson in 1882, Rev. S. T. Anderson, D.D., was acting president for one year. In 1883 Rev. B. G. McLeskey, D.D., formerly of Tennessee but at that time pastor of the church at Sherman, Texas, a graduate of Bethel College, McKenzie,

Rev. E. B. Crisman, D.D.
Financial Agent for
Trinity University
1880-88

Rev. B. G.
McLeskey, D.D.
President of Trinity
University 1883-85

Tennessee, was called to the presidency of Trinity. His career was brief, but his administration was an eminently successful one. He initiated the movement for the completion of the administration building, though the actual work was not begun until 1886 and was not completed until 1892. He died in October, 1885.

Prof. Luther A. Johnson served as president from the death of Dr. McLeskey until 1889 when he resigned. He was succeeded by Rev. J. L. Dickens, Ph.D., who was called from the presidency of Bethel College to this position. He resigned after one year.

In 1890 Rev. B. D. Cockrill was elected president and served for six years. He was born in Kentucky May 28, 1849. He became a Christian and entered the ministry early in life, and rendered a great service as a pastor, particularly at Louisville, Kentucky, where he organized a small congregation of twenty-five members and in the four years just prior to his coming to Trinity University had built it up to a self-sustaining congregation.

From 1896 until 1900 the school continued without a president, but with Professor L. A. Johnson as chairman of the faculty.

Trinity University was not without its financial difficulties. The board had counted on erecting the necessary buildings from the sale of the real estate which had been donated to secure the location of the school at Tehuacana, but soon after the launching of the enterprise the country experienced an unusual shrinkage of values, so much of the necessary funds for building purposes, as well as endowment, had to be secured by donations. Among those who served as financial agents from the beginning of the school until its removal from Tehuacana in 1900 were J. H. Wofford, D. W. Broughton, J. B. Renfro, A. J. Haynes, W. D. Wear, F. E. Foster, J. W. Riggins, S. E. Black, E. B. Crisman, J. W. Pearson, J. M. Halsell, W. J. Lackey, and E. G. McLean.

The work of Rev. E. B. Crisman, D.D., in connection with Trinity University deserves special mention. He served as financial agent for eight years, from 1880 to 1888, combining with this work for fifteen months the pastorate of the church at Corsicana, and for two years occupying the chair of Biblical and Homiletic Instruction. In appreciation of his learning and merit, the degree of Doctor of Divinity was conferred on him by this institution. Though a native of Tennessee where he was born October 1, 1831, he gave much of his life to the work in Texas. His first work in Texas was with the Austin church, 1853-57. Then after an absence of some years during which he was superintendent and corresponding secretary of the Assembly's Board of Missions, located at St. Louis, he came back to Texas, and it was during this period that he was connected with Trinity University. He then returned to Tennessee, but in 1898 came back to Texas to take the pastorate of the churches at Groesbeck, Fairview, and Kosse, which he served until his death February 13, 1899. He was also a writer of note, the best known among his works being his Origin and Doctrines of the Cumberland Presbyterian Church, which passed through three editions and had a circulation of twenty thousand.

As to his success as financial agent for Trinity University, reports show that during the eight years he served in that capacity the productive endowment was increased from $2,146.00 to $29,410.25; non-productive endowment from $19,355.00 to $47,404.80; property from $28,600.00 to $50,541.07, a part of the addition to the administration building having been made during that time. (Minutes of Texas Synod, 1888.)

Rev. John William Pearson, who was financial agent in 1888-89, was born in Alabama, September 8, 1852, the son of Zechariah and Elizabeth Pearson. This parallelism to the names of the parents of John the Baptist was always a source of joy to him. He came to Texas when seventeen or eighteen years of age, secured work in Austin, and remained in that section of the state for a number of years. He joined the Cumberland Presbyterian Church in Williamson County. He came to Tehuacana as a student in Trinity University about 1875 and graduated with high honors. After several years spent in the active ministry, he served as financial agent for Trinity University and later as a member of the board of trustees. In 1909 he was chosen to head the Prohibition ticket as its candidate for governor of Texas. The number of votes recorded was so surprising as to constitute a tribute to his personal influence. He later held pastorates at Richardson, Gainesville, and other points. He was the first president of Cumberland College, which was established at Leonard, Texas, in 1913, and was appointed a member of the Cumberland Presbyterian Educational Endowment Commission in 1918. He and Mrs. Pearson, who was formerly Miss Kittie George and who lived at Tehuacana prior to her marriage in 1886, now make their home at Tehuacana, enjoying the love and devotion of family, neighbors, and friends.

With the completion of the administration building in 1892, the school property, including campus and buildings, was estimated to be worth $84,000. Rev. J. M. Halsell was financial agent when the building was finally completed.

From within the walls of Trinity University, during the sixty-seven years of its existence, there have gone forth hundreds of men and women who have occupied, and are now occupying, places of honor in the various walks of life. Although Trinity is now under the control of another denomination, she stands today a monument to the vision and self-sacrificing labors of Cumberland Presbyterians who made her existence possible. Neither will her influence cease to live on in the Cumberland Presbyterian Church so long as the influence of those who have been won to Christ under the ministry of her students shall live.

### MINISTERS AND CHURCHES IN LITTLE RIVER PRESBYTERY

Rev. R. O. Watkins, who was located at Bosqueville (then in the bounds of Little River Presbytery) in 1860, tells of attending his first meeting of Little River Presbytery on Cowhouse Creek. Members of the presbytery had to carry their guns and pistols with them all the time while presbytery was in session, as the whole country was in a state of alarm because of Indian depredations. He also mentions preaching at Salado Springs and Akin on the Leon, and spent some time in a meeting at "Roundrock campground," in the course of his travels over the country attending presbytery and synod, so it is evident that congregations had been organized at these places at a very early date.

Among the first ministers to locate in Williamson County was Rev. Lewis G. Tucker. He was born in Maury County, Tennessee, January 12, 1811. At the age of twenty-five he was converted and joined the Cumberland Presbyterian Church. At this time he was teaching school, but immediately realizing his call he entered the ministry. In 1836 he married Hannah Rhea, Stephen F. Austin's first cousin.

In October, 1857, they reached Texas and camped north of Austin at Pond Springs. Brown Davis, a colony builder, hearing about the new family rode over to their camp and extended an invitation to them to locate with him at old Block House, a fort built (and occupied by a few families) to protect the early settlers. Upon learning that Tucker was a Cumberland Presbyterian minister, Mr. Davis was more eager than ever to get him to locate with them and hold services. The meeting between the Davis and Tucker families was like a family reunion, as both were Cumberland Presbyterians. This was the first Cumberland Presbyterian sermon preached in this part of Texas. Soon afterward a church was organized with twelve members and was called Pond Springs.

Later he moved fourteen miles west of Georgetown on a farm which he cultivated for a living, while he preached over a territory in a radius of sixty miles of his home. He always traveled by horseback, and in his saddle bag could be found the Holy Bible, a hymn book, and clean socks and shirt which were ever ready through the faithful help of his devoted wife. He organized churches at Pond Springs (known now as

Pleasant Hill), Elm Grove (known now as Oak Grove), Hopewell, and Hudson's Bend.

With regard to the early history of Elm Grove, which was located in the community where the Tuckers lived, the following incident is related. Located in the same community was another Cumberland Presbyterian family named Matsler, and it was through Mrs. Matsler's influence, together with the help of the Tucker family, that a Sunday school was organized. Another Cumberland Presbyterian minister, Rev. W. R. Bauchman, also moved into this community, and it was decided among them that they should build a church. While they were hewing the logs an intruder came along and demanded to know if they realized whose timber they were using. Mr. Matsler who was overseeing the job remarked that he "didn't suppose it mattered." Some curt words were exchanged, and Bauchman, realizing that trouble was close at hand, yelled out, "Hold on, Brother Matsler, I'll fix him," as he rolled up his sleeves with ax in hand, whereupon the intruder took to flight. There was no further interference, and the log church was completed. Rev. L. G. Tucker died in 1880.

In the minutes of Little River Presbytery for December, 1883, there is a petition from a group of members of the Elm Grove congregation asking that the congregation be divided into two congregations. This was done, and a new congregation was organized known as Pilot Knob, which was in existence for a number of years. Evidently this congregation and Elm Grove were later united to form the Oak Grove congregation.

Rev. R. B. (Bob) Davis, who was one of the greatest pulpit orators this part of Texas ever knew, spent his life in Williamson, Bell, and Burnet Counties. He was for many years stated clerk of Little River Presbytery.

Rev. John Hudson was ordained by Little River Presbytery in 1859 and worked in Bell, Williamson, and San Saba Counties in Indian times. He afterward spent some time in Missouri, returning to Little River Presbytery in 1874 or 1875. He preached for a number of years at Round Rock and Hutto. His ministry also extended north into Lampasas and Mills Counties.

Rev. W. R. Bauchman entered the ministry late in life, but accomplished a great work for the church. His work was principally in Williamson, Bell, and Milam Counties, and he also organized the Shady Grove church in Burnet County, July, 1878.

Rev. B. E. Bowmer was born at Round Rock, Williamson County, May 13, 1854. He was converted in 1870 at the old Live Oak camp ground, under the ministry of Rev. J. J. A. Roach, and was received under the care of Little River Presbytery as a candidate for the ministry in 1875. His first year in the active ministry was spent as a missionary over a territory embracing Burnet, Lampasas, Llano, and other counties to the west, in which he laid the foundation for churches which were afterward established. In Little River Presbytery he held pastorates in Burnet, Williamson, Lampasas, and Llano Counties. One of his longest pastorates included the Mt. Zion and Shady Grove churches in Burnet County. He was a strong advocate of the grouping system which was used very successfully in Little River Presbytery for a number of years in supplying the churches with preaching.

Later his ministry extended westward to San Saba and Tom Green Counties. In more recent years he has held a number of pastorates in the north, central, and eastern portions of the state, among which were Hubbard, Ferris, and a pastorate in East Texas embracing Hope Chapel, Pine Tree, and Elmira Chapel.

REV. AND MRS. B. E. BOWMER

He has held revival meetings all over Texas and Louisiana. Over a period of sixty years dating back to the time when the preachers had to carry six-shooters to defend themselves from hostile Indians, there is probably no other man who has labored more extensively in the interest of the Cumberland Presbyterian Church in Texas than he. Since 1913 he has been stated clerk of Texas Synod.

Rev. S. C. Lockett was born in Arkansas, but came to Texas as a child. His name first appears on the directory of Little River Presbytery as an ordained minister in the year 1882. His home was in Burnet County near Bertram where he began publishing a paper which was afterward known as Our Church Helper.

Other men were connected with the church in Little River Presbytery at an earlier date whose work lay in the territory out of which the presbyteries of Waco and San Saba were formed. The work of some of these will be considered in the account of those presbyteries.

### WACO PRESBYTERY

Several congregations had been organized before 1860 in the vicinity of Waco, which was at that time in the bounds of Little River Presbytery. From the diary of Rev. R. O. Watkins, who lived at Bosqueville during the year 1860, we learn that he preached to the Bosqueville and Waco churches and to another church called Concord. At Waco the Cumberland Presbyterian congregation had the use of the Methodist church for its services the third Sunday in each month. In August of that year Watkins held a protracted meeting at Clifton, in Bosque County. He also mentions a Rev. John Smith, with whom he was associated in the ministry and who was pastor of a church known as Ramsey's Creek.

Rock Church, in Bosque County, was organized October 16, 1864. Among the pioneers of Bosque County who helped establish this church were the Odles and Standifers.

Alfred Chandler Odle, who was for many years an

elder and clerk of the session at Rock Church, was born in Fannin County May 6, 1845, and moved with his parents to Bosque County in 1866. He helped to haul the rock to build the church. Miss Aura Amanda Barton, who later became his wife, also joined this congregation in 1866.

John Hogue Standifer came from Alabama and settled in Bosque County in 1865. He had been made an elder in the church in Alabama in 1851, when he was twenty-four years of age. His wife, who was formerly Miss Martha Swinney, was of a family of strong Cumberland Presbyterians of Cherokee County, Alabama, to whom the Rev. Robert Donnell had ministered. J. H. Standifer became a leader in the religious activities at Rock Church and served for many years as superintendent of the Sunday school. He attended camp meeting at Rock Church twenty-four years in succession, camping each year on the same spot. When he was eighty-four years of age, being unable to attend presbytery, he petitioned the presbytery to grant him a license to exhort. The presbytery granted him a license to preach instead. He died January 30, 1915. A son, S. R. Standifer, and a grandson, S. R. Estes, are ministers in the Cumberland Presbyterian Church.

In 1874 the Colorado Synod cut off this portion of Little River Presbytery to form a new presbytery, which was called Bosque Presbytery. Rev. O. A. Lackey (father of Revs. W. J. and J. A. Lackey) was appointed by the synod as the first moderator. The first directory of this presbytery published in the minutes of the General Assembly, that of 1875, lists the following ordained ministers as members of Bosque Presbytery: F. C. Baker, R. H. Castleman,

Jesse Estelle, J. C. Gaston, E. J. Gillespie, D. C. Kinnard (stated clerk), O. A. Lackey, J. Phillips, and John Reed. W. J. Lackey is listed as a candidate. Two years after its organization the name of this presbytery was changed to Waco.

A number of strong congregations were built up, particularly in Bosque, Coryell, and Hamilton Counties, and other able ministers were added to the ranks of this presbytery. The union disturbance left this presbytery destitute of preachers. Only a bare quorum remained, and two of these three ministers were past the age of activity in the ministry, so in 1910 Waco Presbytery was consolidated with Corsicana Presbytery. Only three congregations out of what had been Waco Presbytery were ever enrolled in the consolidated presbytery. This field is one which has been neglected in recent years. There are said to be many Cumberland Presbyterians scattered over this territory. They should be looked after.

## SAN SABA PRESBYTERY

On the first page of the session records of the Harmony Ridge congregation is the record of the organization, August 23, 1857, of a Cumberland Presbyterian church with nine members. This congregation was organized by Rev. W. B. Wear, an ordained minister of Little River Presbytery, and went by the name of San Saba. F. M. Harrel and E. D. Sutton were the first elders. The first minutes of the session are signed by John Hudson, clerk of the session. John Hudson, who afterward became a noted preacher in Little River Prebytery, was engaged in teaching school about that time, and in 1860-61 served a term as county clerk of

San Saba County. He and his wife, who before her marriage was Miss Canzadie A. Hamilton, were among the charter members of this organization. Although the name and perhaps the location of this congregation were afterward changed, this first Cumberland Presbyterian church ever organized in San Saba County, and probably the first in the territory later occupied by San Saba Presbytery, is perpetuated until today in the Harmony Ridge congregation. A few years later churches were organized at Rock Shoals and Wallace Creek, above the town of San Saba.

The first regular pastor of Cumberland Presbyterian churches in San Saba County was Rev. S. M. Lewis. He came to Texas in 1855 from Talladega Presbytery, Alabama, and settled in Caldwell County. In 1858 he established a school at Lampasas which was in operation four years until interrupted by the Civil War. He then entered the Confederate army as a chaplain. Returning from the war he made his home in San Saba County, preaching at Harmony Ridge, Rock Shoals, and other points. He resided in this county until his death in January, 1899, and was buried in the Harmony Ridge cemetery.

It was he who helped to establish the Harmony Ridge community in the bend of the San Saba River near where that stream flows into the Colorado. After several had settled there it was decided to erect a schoolhouse, and when the house was finished they gathered to name the community. Mr. John Kimbrough said he had never seen so much harmony among so great a number working together as he had seen in the erection of that schoolhouse, and as the schoolhouse was situated upon a ridge he suggested

that it be called Harmony Ridge. The church building, which was later used for both school and church
purposes, was erected on land donated by the three
Oliver brothers—Mark, Andrew, and Polk Oliver—who
settled in the community in 1882. All of them were
elders in the Cumberland Presbyterian Church and
contributed much to the progress of the church after
they came to this community. Each of these brothers
reared a large family, and members of the Oliver
family are still prominently connected with the church,
not only in San Saba County, but elsewhere. There
are, at the present time, four Olivers who are elders
in the Harmony Ridge and San Saba churches.

San Saba Presbytery was formed by order of Colorado Synod in 1881. According to the directory appearing in the General Assembly minutes of the following year, the ministers composing this presbytery
were Revs. Z. T. Blanton, J. S. Boatright, T. A. Ish,
F. E. Lawler, S. M. Lewis, J. A. Robinson (stated
clerk), W. C. Sparks, and R. D. Wear. This presbytery embraced a large territory extending westward
indefinitely. In those days when presbytery would
meet on the extreme western porder it would take
four or five days for some of the brethren to go to
presbytery.

A church was organized in the early eighties at
Brownwood with thirteen charter members. Among
the first pastors of this church was Rev. R. W. Lewis,
a young man who had recently come to Texas from
Mississippi and was called to Brownwood in the spring
of 1885. He had been licensed by Lebanon Presbytery
while attending Cumberland University, but was not
yet ordained.

Soon after locating there he got Dixon C. Williams, the lay evangelist from Lebanon, Tennessee, to come and hold a tent meeting. He came in a stage, jumped out at the first saloon (there were seven in the town), told the driver to wait on him; ran in and hugged the saloon-keeper, invited all in the saloon to hear him that night, jumped back in the stage and told the driver to take him to every saloon in town. This was done, and all the saloon men were invited to come out that night. Among the first converts of the meeting was the wife of the keeper of the saloon where Williams did the hugging act. A number of the most prominent men in town, such as the newspaper editor, bankers, cattle kings (at least three of these), and a leading horse ranchman were converted, and a number of them joined the Cumberland Presbyterian Church. It was not long until a brick church was under construction, these cattle men putting in their money by the thousands. During this meeting Rev. Alpha Young came in his buggy from Buffalo Gap, a distance of ninety miles. He never ceased to marvel at the uniqueness, the freshness, the many verses read from the Bible in each sermon, the crowds that came, the scores who went night after night to the altar, and the strong men who were saved.

R. W. Lewis preached also at Coleman and at Santa Anna, where he arranged for the organization of churches, but not being ordained as yet, he had Rev. A. J. Haynes to come from Buffalo Gap to officiate in the organization. In the Santa Anna congregation which was organized in May, 1885, were four Kirkpatrick brothers—Thomas, George, Andrew, and Robert Donnell—who had moved to this part of the country from Ellis County. They were sons of Rev. W. J. Kirkpatrick, a Cumberland Presbyterian minister. They and the family of R. F. Campbell had been members of the old Kirkpatrick church in Ellis County where "Uncle Jack" Haynes had ministered before he, too, had come west. George F. Kirkpatrick served as a ruling elder from before his removal to Coleman County until his death in January, 1913.

In 1885 Rev. J. B. Wright came up from Guadalupe Presbytery and the following year settled on the McCulloch County side of the Colorado River and united with San Saba Presbytery. He remained a member of this presbytery continuously until his death in 1932. He was for fifteen years pastor of the Santa Anna church, and organized and preached to several congregations in Coleman and McCulloch Counties, among them Trickham, and a church near where he lived, called Riverside. He was a graduate of Trinity University, and though qualified from an educational standpoint to have held a more prominent place, he chose to remain on the frontier. As a pastor he was greatly loved by his people. As a presbyter, though a man of strong convictions, he had the rare quality of being able to suggest ways and means of adjusting those differences which frequently arise as a result of misunderstanding. He served as moderator of more sessions of this presbytery than any other man. When troublesome questions were about to come before the presbytery he was the man sought out to serve as moderator.

Rev. W. H. White came into San Saba Presbytery about the same time. He had been president of Buffalo Gap College, and in 1886 retired from that position and went to Sherwood, in Irion County, where he taught school and preached. When not engaged in teaching he would drill water wells for a living while ministering to the sparsely settled communities on the frontier of Southwest Texas. During the time of his residence at Sherwood he organized the South Concho congregation where Christoval now stands, and led in the erection of a church building at that place.

Rev. E. D. Dysart, a graduate of Trinity University and formerly of Red River Presbytery, became pastor of the Ballinger and Coleman churches in about 1890. While thus engaged he organized a small group of Cumberland Presbyterians at San Angelo into a congregation to which he preached once a month until the church grew sufficiently to locate a man there. In 1900 and 1901 he served the San Saba group and during his pastorate a manse was built.

Among others who had a part in building up the church in this field during the early days of San Saba Presbytery were Revs. B. E. Bowmer, F. M. Gilliam (who from about 1890 until his death in 1905 was stated clerk of the presbytery), and J. B. Atkinson.

The name of this presbytery was changed to Brownwood in 1902. In the meantime a strong presbytery had been built up and good churches established in most of the principal towns. All of the stronger churches were eventually lost to the Cumberland Church, however, in the confusion accompanying the attempted union with the Presbyterian Church, U. S. A., in 1906. Discouragement followed; the older ministers who for many years held the presbytery together passed on; and in 1934 Brownwood Presbytery, with the exception of one congregation in the western part which was added to Amarillo Presbytery, was consolidated with Austin Presbytery.  More than once the prospect of maintaining the churches which remained has seemed dark.  However, there has recently been a revival of interest in a number of the churches which is encouraging.  A missionary is now at work in that field.  This is a large territory and there are many Cumberland Presbyterians scattered over it.  It is a field which the church cannot afford to abandon.

### BUFFALO GAP PRESBYTERY

In 1884 Colorado Synod ordered the formation of a new presbytery to be known as Buffalo Gap Presbytery.  According to the first directory which appears in the General Assembly minutes, that of 1886, the ordained ministers composing this presbytery were Revs. O. W. Carter, A. J. Haynes, J. R. Hodges, D. A. Knox, F. E. Leech, W. H. White, and Alpha Young.  In 1895 the name was changed to Abilene Presbytery.

### EARLY HISTORY OF THE TAYLOR STREET CHURCH, FORT WORTH*

In June, 1878, Rev. A. H. Stephens, a young Cumberland Presbyterian preacher not yet ordained, who had just graduated from Trinity University at Tehuacana, Texas, was employed by the St. Louis Observer, a new Cumberland Presbyterian paper, to canvas for the paper in the region around Fort Worth.  Equipped with a good cow pony, a Bible, and an old fashioned hymn book,

---

*The details relative to the beginning of the first Cumberland Presbyterian church in Fort Worth were contributed by the minister who led in establishing this church, Rev. A. H. Stephens, now of Warrensburg, Mo.

he started out with the purpose of preaching at night in the schoolhouses and canvassing for his paper during the day.

On a certain Saturday night he blew into Fort Worth, which was then a border town of about three thousand people, and on inquiring as to where he could stay all night, he was directed to a Mr. Daniels, who kept a boarding house. In the conversation which followed, he found out that Mr. and Mrs. Daniels were from Clarksville, Missouri, and were Cumberland Presbyterians. On finding out that his guest expected to be a preacher, Mr. Daniels said, "Well, if you are to be a preacher, why not preach for us tomorrow?" The invitation was accepted, and a place secured for the service in a public hall on Houston Street.

Quite a little group of people, about one dozen in number, assembled for the Sunday morning service, among them Mr. W. T. Fakes, a Mr. Foster, a Mrs. Turner, a Mr. Buchanan and family, and Mr. and Mrs. Daniels. At the conclusion of the service Mr. Fakes, who was from Lebanon, Tennessee, Mr. Daniels, and some others asked if he could not preach again that night. He did, and there were about twenty-five people came.

After a hurried conference, the little group inquired whether the young preacher could stay and preach for them all the time. He said he thought he could, that he "could stand it if they could." All seemed to be at a loss as to salary, but Mr. and Mrs. Daniels said, "We will give him his board." So the young preacher accepted the proposition, having in view to work the paper business during the week and make a little money so he could ride the street cars. Fort Worth then had

a mule line from the court house to the Texas and Pacific depot, the T&P being the only railroad in Fort
Worth at the time.

After worshiping for some time in the hall on Houston Street, the owner raised the rent, so the congregation decided to use a schoolhouse out in the southwest
part of town, which would cost nothing. In this schoolhouse the church was organized with fifteen charter
members.

Soon the congregation determined to undertake the
work of building a new church. The young preacher
went out among the cattle men where he had made
many new friends, and secured donations of cattle, hogs,
and other live stock. Others volunteered to bring in
all the stock, and a few days later the motley herd of
live stock—cattle, hogs, and sheep—were brought into
town to be sold. Soon the entire lot was sold out, and
fifteen hundred dollars was in the treasury of the little
church.

A lot on the corner of Fifth and Taylor Streets was
donated by a Mr. Buchanan, one of the members; others donated labor, and within a few weeks the little
white church was completed. In the new church house
the congregation grew. After eleven months spent in
Fort Worth in this rather novel enterprise, the young
preacher went to Lebanon, Tennessee, to continue his
studies in the theological seminary. Soon the town began to grow, railroads were built, wealthy men came,
and among them many Cumberland Presbyterians. Under the ministry of Dr. R. M. Tinnon, who became pastor in 1886, a new stone building was erected.

It was here, while Dr. Tinnon was pastor of this
church, that Gam Sing Quah, who is now and has been

for twenty-eight years superintendent of our mission work in South China, was converted. Thus has the influence of the little church, planted under such unusual circumstances, reached unto "the uttermost part of the earth."

## PARSONS PRESBYTERY

From the most reliable information obtainable, it is generally understood that a Cumberland Presbyterian church was organized in Weatherford in 1859. Rev. Reuben Sanders was pastor before the Civil War. Red Oak Presbytery, which then embraced that territory, met in Weatherford in 1863. Rev. C. W. Berry, who came up from Mansfield, preached at Weatherford and other points in Parker County beginning in 1866. In 1869 Rev. G. W. Parsons became pastor of the Weatherford church and preached there until the spring of 1872. He was killed accidentally while out turkey hunting. After his death Rev. B. D. Austin served the church for a time, and was followed by his brother, Rev. W. B. Austin. The church was thrown into a confused state by the sudden disappearance of the session clerk and all of the church records, but on March 12, 1875, was reorganized by Rev. Aaron Griggsby.

The Spring Creek church was organized by Rev. Samuel Ezell March 15, 1874, with twenty members. Other churches had been organized in Parker County and adjacent territory by this time. Thus the foundation was laid for a new presbytery which was created in 1877 by the Brazos Synod, and which was known as Graham Presbytery. Two years later the name was changed to Parsons Presbytery in memory of Rev. W. G. Parsons.

The early records of Parsons Presbytery indicate that it was a live and growing organization, although it was principally made up of rural churches of small membership, and the preachers labored with but little financial support from the churches. One minister in making his report to presbytery for the year 1887 mentions having received from one congregation "the shoeing of one horse and fifty cents." Most of the churches paid some more than that, but as a rule the salaries were very small.

A vital missionary zeal was manifested on the part of the ministry. New churches were reported frequently. Rev. E. V. Butler was employed for some time as presbyterial missionary. On another occasion when certain places, mostly schoolhouses, were mentioned as prospective points for the organization of churches, candidates and licentiates were designated to preach at those places until the next meeting of the presbytery. This presbytery also established and maintained for a period of several years a high school at Veal's Station, Parker County, known as Parsons High School.

In 1901 the name of this presbytery was changed to Weatherford.

Of the charter members of Parsons Presbytery, Rev. G. W. Rushing spent a longer ministry in its bounds than any other man. He was born at White House, Rusk County, August 11, 1848, but in his boyhood moved to Kaufman County where he lived until after he was married. His early life was spent on the farm and clerking in a store. In the year 1872 he was converted and united with the Cumberland Presbyterian Church and in the same year he came under the care of presbytery as a candidate for the ministry and entered school. He was ordained a year or two later, and had an active ministry of fifty-three years, during which time he missed only two meetings of his presbytery. He moved to Parker County in 1877 and organized a church at the Wright schoolhouse, to which congregation he preached once a month for twenty-one years. He devoted the remainder of his time to farming, school teaching, holding revival meetings, and organizing churches. Among the congregations he is known to have organized were Peaster, Mary's Creek and Erwin schoolhouse, in Parker County, and Megargel and Cottonwood in Archer County. In 1897 he moved to Olney to serve as pastor of the Olney church which pastorate he held for twelve consecutive years. He passed away September 8, 1925, and his remains were laid to rest in the new Olney cemetery.

## HISTORY OF THE OLNEY CHURCH

The pioneer Cumberland Presbyterian minister of Young County was Rev. E. V. Butler. Church records of early Cumberland Presbyterian churches in the Olney territory now in possession of the Olney church show that Rev. E. V. Butler organized a church at Graham October 12, 1876, another known as Hufstuttle December 3, 1892, and another known as Cottonwood July 13, 1889. It was the Cottonwood church out of which the Olney church grew. The charter members of this congregation were J. W. Groves, J. H. Davidson, L. Davidson, M. A. Davidson, T. Kenedy, B. Davidson, S. H. Splawn, R. B. Neeley, A. C. Neeley, H. E. Neeley, F. S. Groves, and Katie Splawn. J. W. Groves and J. H. Davidson were elders. Of the members who originally made up this church, H. E. Neeley is the only one who is now a member of the Olney congregation.

In August, 1891, a joint camp meeting was held with the Methodists which was evidently a very successful meeting, as some twenty new members were added to the Cumberland Presbyterian Church. This meeting was conducted by Rev. E. V. Butler, pastor of the Cumberland Presbyterian church, and Rev. E. W. Simmons, the Methodist minister.

Records show that the name of this congregation was officially changed to Olney on October 21, 1891. This church made rapid progress and soon grew to be a strong congregation which through the years has exerted a great influence upon the spiritual life of the community. A number of able ministers have served this church, the entire list being Revs. E. V. Butler, G. W. Rushing, C. W. Dunn, W. Y. Durrett, W. A. Clack, B. E. Bowmer, H. G. Nicholson, H. H. Green, W. J. Walker, J. L. Elliott, W. R. Harber, J. A. Rodgers, R. E. Matlock, O. A. Mealor, J. F. Walton, Paul F. Brown, and H. H. Hunter.

In 1926 the new brick church building was erected at a cost of about twenty-three thousand dollars. This congregation has been host to Texas Synod a number of times, and in 1930 was host to the One Hundredth General Assembly of the Cumberland Presbyterian Church. In the changing of presbyterial lines, Olney was transferred to Gregory Presbytery in 1927.

Another congregation bearing the name of Cottonwood was organized by Rev. G. W. Rushing in 1910, but this organization was later dissolved and transferred to the Olney church, as were several other small organizations in this vicinity.

## TRINITY SYNOD

In 1878, in response to memorials from Texas Synod and members of Brazos Synod, a new synod was formed under the name of Trinity Synod, composed of Guthrie, Graham, and Red Oak Presbyteries. The General Assembly's order provided that this synod "hold its first meeting with Flower Mound church, in Denton County, Texas, on Thursday before the second Sabbath in October, 1878, at 7 o'clock p. m., and that Rev. A. S. Hayter be the first moderator, and Rev. D. R. Grafton his alternate." This synod was formed as ordered, thus making four synods lying wholly or partially within the state of Texas.

## GREGORY PRESBYTERY

In the summer of 1860 Rev. John Overton Parr, who was then living in Grayson County, went with a party of surveyors to locate some land on the head of Big Sandy west of where Bowie now is. Being there over Sunday, he got what settlers were there and the surveying party together and preached to them. This was probably the first sermon preached by a Cumberland Presbyterian in that part of the country.

In 1876 Rev. W. J. Gregory, who had been a pioneer preacher in Denton County, again sought the frontier and purchased a farm in the northwestern part of Wise County, near Chico, to which he moved. Here he resumed his church work, organized the first church in the village of Chico, and was its pastor for thirteen years. His ministry was extended westward into Jack County, also.

It has been said that perhaps no life in Northwest Texas surpassed in the extent and effectiveness of its labors that of Rev. W. J. Gregory. He was born in Nelson County, Kentucky, November 29, 1820, and on November 28, 1839, was married to Miss Millie Grundy. At the age of eighteen he was converted and joined the Cumberland Presbyterian Church and was immediately impressed with a call to the ministry. Though his opportunities for securing an education were limited, as his father had died when he was about two years of age, through hard study he acquired a good practical education and became a strong preacher and a profound theologian. He came to Texas in 1852 and located first in Grayson County, moving later to Cooke and Denton Counties where he engaged regularly in church work until he moved to Wise County and planted the Cumberland Presbyterian Church in that part of the country. He remained there until his death which occurred when his home caught fire and he was entrapped in the flames.

In 1878 Rev. W. C. Walker came to Texas from the pastorate of the Savannah, Tennessee, and other nearby churches, and settled at Newport, in Clay County, seventy-five miles northwest of Fort Worth which was then the nearest railroad station. In March, 1880, he organized the Cumberland Presbyterian Church at Newport with twenty-two members. The first elders were S. M. King, T. J. Walker, and W. M. Wagoner. At that time there were no churches west of Newport and none for many miles east. Of the members who originally composed this congregation, so far as is known, Rev. W. J. Walker, son of Rev. W. C. Walker, is the only one now living. Rev. W. C. Walker served as pastor of this congregation until 1891 when Rev. W. J. Walker became pastor, who served until failing health forced his retirement in 1933.

The records of the Newport church show that on May 20, 1893, this congregation decided to build its first house of worship, which was accomplished under the leadership of F. B. Bulls, father of Ed F. Bulls who is now, and has been for many years, an elder in that congregation.

Rev. W. C. Walker blazed the trail for the spread of the Cumberland Presbyterian Church throughout that section and organized many of the churches existing today. In the meantime, other ministers located in that region, among whom were Revs. W. R. Baker and J. W. Reid, whose work was principally in Montague County, and Rev. W. B. Austin who in 1885 organized the Zion Valley congregation in Wise County. This territory was then a part of Guthrie Presbytery, which included Denton and Cooke Counties and extended westward indefinitely.

At the meeting of Trinity Synod held at Flower Mound, Denton County, in the fall of 1882, an order was passed, through the efforts of Rev. W. C. Walker, for the formation of a new presbytery, and Rev. W. J. Gregory was appointed moderator.

This new presbytery was organized Thursday night, March 22, 1883, at the Cottonwood church west of Montague, and was named Gregory Presbytery in honor of its first moderator, the man who organized many of its churches. The members of Gregory Pres-

bytery present at its organization were Revs. W. J.
Gregory, W. C. Walker, W. B. Austin, C. C. Upton,
and J. W. Reid. Members absent were Revs. J. J.
Armor, W. R. Baker, and J. N. Brunson. This presbytery has functioned regularly since its organization.

When Gregory Presbytery was organized its territory included parts of Montague and Wise Counties
and all of Northwest Texas. Later a presbytery was
organized on its Western border known as Pease
River, now Amarillo.

### KIRKPATRICK PRESBYTERY

Kirkpatrick Presbytery was formed by the Brazos
Synod in 1875 out of parts of the presbyteries of Red
Oak and Tehuacana. It was named in honor of Rev.
William J. Kirkpatrick who had formerly labored in its
bounds. According to the directory appearing in the
General Assembly minutes of 1876, the ministers com-
posing this presbytery were Revs. Wil'is Burgess, Jere-
miah Cunningham, R. B. Groves, William H. Groves,
Y. H. Hamilton, James Johnson, J. M. Kerr, W. G. L.
Quaite, J. W. Smith, J. A. Ward, and Alpha Young.

As to the older churches in this presbytery, we have
already given a history of the Corsicana church. Another old church was Liberty Hill, located in the western part of Navarro County. This church was organized by Rev. R. B. Groves December 23, 1860, with thirteen charter members. The records indicate that the
members of this congregation were formerly members
of the Richland congregation. The first elders were
Samuel Wright and William Fullerton. Rev. Willis
Burgess preached to this congregation for quite a while

during the early seventies. This church was in existence until about eight years ago when the congregation disbanded, most of the members uniting with the church at Hubbard.

Henry Groves, an elder in the Cumberland Presbyterian Church from Illinois, settled in the vicinity of where Milford now is in the year 1853. Soon afterward the congregation which later became known as Milford was organized in his home by Rev. Finis E. King. This Groves family produced several preachers. The Rev. J. Sanford Groves, for many years pastor at Mexia, and Rev. R. B. Groves were sons of Henry Groves.

## BONHAM PRESBYTERY

Bonham Presbytery was formed by Texas Synod in 1883. There is evidence of the existence of Cumberland Presbyterian churches at Sherman, Bonham, and Honey Grove at a very early day. Another old congregation which came within the bounds of this presbytery was Oak Hill, later known as Grove Hill, which was organized by Rev. William R. Baker September 11, 1864. Among the charter members were E. S. Groves and wife, parents of W. L. Groves and the late John W. Groves of Olney. This congregation existed until a few years ago. Rev. G. L. Waddle was reared in this community and was converted while plowing for W. L. Groves during a revival held under an old time brush arbor at Grove Hill. Bonham Presbytery was a strong presbytery for many years.

## BUFFALO GAP COLLEGE

This institution was founded in 1882 at Buffalo Gap, Taylor County, Texas, through the efforts of Revs. A. J.

Haynes and Alpha Young. Buffalo Gap is situated about fourteen miles southwest of Abilene in a range of hills which at this particular place attain to a height of three or four hundred feet above the surrounding prairie. This range constitutes the watershed between the Brazos and Colorado Rivers. It is said that Buffalo Gap derived its name from the fact that the main trial from north to south which was traveled by the herds of buffalo that formerly inhabited this region used to pass through this gap. The location was a very healthful one, the climate being dry and the altitude of the town about 1,900 feet above sea level. When the school was located there the Texas and Pacific Railroad had not been built as far west as Abilene, and Buffalo Gap was the county seat of Taylor County.

Rev. A. J. Haynes served as financial agent in raising the money to launch the enterprise, and Rev. Alpha Young superintended the erection of the building, which was a red sandstone structure capable of accommodating three hundred pupils. It will be remembered that both of these men had served in like capacities in the early days of Trinity University, and now with the indomitable courage and energy characteristic of the West, they set out to establish an institution of learning to serve as an educational center on the advancing frontier.

The school opened in the fall of 1882 under the leadership of Professor J. N. Ellis as president. Other instructors were Professor Taylor, Miss Belle Young, and Miss Eudona Haynes (now Mrs. J. D. Cullum) music teacher.

In 1884 Rev. W. H. White became president of the school. He was a native of Rutherford County, Tennes-

Rev. W. H. White

Rev. A. J. Haynes

Rev. Alpha Young

see, where he was born November 16, 1844. He entered the ministry of the Cumberland Presbyterian Church in Elk Presbytery soon after the Civil War, and became an outstanding scholar and teacher as well as rendering a great service as a preacher, particularly as a missionary on the frontier. He came to Texas in 1880 and was attending the meeting of Bacon Presbytery, of which he was a member, when word reached the presbytery concerning the vacancy in Buffalo Gap College. The presbytery immediately passed a resolution recommending him for the presidency of that institution. Associated with him as a teacher in Buffalo Gap College from 1884 to 1886 was Mr. J. W. Christopher, a brother-in-law, who was also a native of Tennessee, having been born near Eagleville, Tennessee, in the year 1845.

Rev. Mr. White's administration was an eminently successful one. The report of this institution as it appears in the Minutes of the General Assembly, 1885, shows an enrollment of one hundred and twenty students, four instructors, and buildings worth $10,000. In its beginning this school was operated as a high school, but the success of the institution and the demands of the country induced the trustees to have it chartered in 1886 as a college, with power to confer degrees. As chartered, this college was owned and controlled jointly by the Buffalo Gap and San Saba Presbyteries, the former electing five trustees, and the latter electing four. The board of trustees in 1886 was composed of E. P. Beauchamp (president) Rev. A. Young (financial agent), P. T. Hurt (secretary), Rev. A. J. Haynes, W. A. Humphreys, D. F. Springfield, Fred Brookreson, W. C. Wylie, W. C. Cheatham, all of Buffalo Gap; P. C. Gamble (treasurer), Abilene; and J. Hathaway, Runnels.

The school, which from the beginning had been a co-educational institution, now offered the degrees of Bachelor of Arts and Bachelor of Science upon completion of the collegiate course. A primary school and a preparatory school were also maintained.

Prominent among the student activities was a Philomathian Literary Society organized in 1885 and chartered under the laws of Texas. This society sponsored the publication of a monthly journal, The Philomathian Palm. The records indicate that it was a live organization.

In 1886 Professor J. M. Wagstaff, formerly of Lynnville, Tennessee, succeeded to the presidency of the school, in which position he served until 1890, when forced to retire on account of ill health. With him were associated Professor Will C. Lasley, Miss Ella Wagstaff, Miss Mamie Walker, and Miss Sallie R. Young. Miss Walker, who was from Missisippi, had charge of the music department in the year 1890. Miss Sallie R. Young, daughter of Rev. Alpha Young, who had charge of the primary department for a number of years, had a notable career as a teacher, having served as instructor in the primary department in Trinity University 1872-1886, and then was for some forty years a teacher at Buffa'o Gap and near by. She was one of the best known teachers in the West.

New names appearing as trustees during this period include Judge T. W. Daugherty and Rev. D. C. DeWitt of Abilene, Rev. R. W. Benge (secretary), Prof. J. M. Wagstaff, and a Mr. Davis of Ballinger.

In 1890 Rev. R. W. Benge, who had been for some

time pastor of the local Cumberland Presbyterian Church, became president of the college and served for two years. Under his administration the enrollment reached a total of 197 in all departments for the year closing June 8, 1892. Other members of the faculty included Mr. John R. Haynes, teacher of mathematics, natural sciences, and German; C. M. Murray, teacher of English, elocution and vocal music and head of the preparatory department; Miss Armine Haynes, teacher of instrumental music; and Miss Sallie R. Young, primary department.

As to the government of the school, included among the regulations listed in the catalogue of 1891 is one which says, "Attending social parties and kindred forms of dissipation is forbidden, except by special permission of the Faculty." A subsequent catalogue adds that "note writing between the sexes is severely punished."

Public examinations, usually covering a period of two days, were held at the close of each session of school, which were attended by visiting committees previously appointed by the two interested presbyteries, who sat in to hear the examinations and report back to their respective presbyteries the kind and grade of work being done by the college.

The following departments were embraced in the collegiate department: English, mathematics, philosophy and history, ancient and modern languages, natural science, music, and Biblical study.

A news item from a county newspaper of the year 1890 refers to Buffalo Gap as "the Athens of the Banner County of the grandest state in this American union."

In the class of 1887 there were four graduates; in 1888, four; in 1889, one; in 1890, five.

Trustees during the years 1891 and 1892 were: for Buffalo Gap Presbytery, Rev. A. J. Haynes, T. W. Daugherty, J. H. Beall, Rev. F. E. Leech, and J. M. Wagstaff; for San Saba Presbytery, Fred Brookreson, B. F. Jones, P. T. Hurt, and J. L. Standifer.

Rev. John Collier became president in 1892 and served for a period of several years. The school continued in a prosperous state, there being in 1898 twelve graduates receiving the bachelor's degree.

In about the year 1900 Rev. W. H. White again succeeded to the presidency, but by that time changing conditions and the extension of the public school system was having its effect on all private and church owned schools which depended upon the local patronage of a primary and preparatory department to keep them going, so after some three years the school was discontinued.

During the twenty or more years of its existence, Buffalo Gap College rendered a great service to the Cumberland Presbyterian Church and to the cause of Christian education in the West. Many useful men and women went out from its walls to take their places as citizens in the various vocations of life. A number of ministerial students also received their training here, among them, M. L. Spence, A. N. Ridenhour, J. T. Bryant, T. R. Mauldin, C. D. Calvert, S. D. Waldrop, N. R. French, and W. M. Bennett.

## OTHER PRESBYTERIAL SCHOOLS

A high school located at Veal's Station, Parker County, and known as Parsons High School, was taken under the care of the Parsons Presbytery in 1881 or 1882. Rev. Luther A. Johnson, who later became president of Trinity University, was its first principal, and Rev. William Piercy assistant. In 1885 Rev. S. E. Kennon became principal and Prof. J. L. Shipley first assistant. Prof. J. C. Hague was principal in 1887, and in later years the school was operated under the administration of W. A. Erwin. This school was short-lived, but did a good work, not only in the training of candidates for the ministry, but in affording to all of its students the wholesome influence of a Christian institution. This school had students from several counties.

In 1893 Red Oak Academy was established at Burleson by the Red Oak Presbytery. Rev. L. C. Collier became its first president and served five years. This school consistently avoided the name college, and confined its work to preparatory courses. It maintained a strong teaching force. In April, 1899, Rev. L. C. Collier resigned, and Prof. J. N. Ellis, a ruling elder in the Cumberland Presbyterian Church, formerly of Buffalo Gap College, was elected president.

## CHURCH PAPERS

Beginning in April, 1873, Revs. J. B. Renfro and J. H. Wofford were associated together in the publication of the Texas Cumberland Presbyterian. Rev. J. B. Renfro soon sold his interest in the paper to Rev. J. H. Wofford, who continued the paper until December, 1874, when the General Assembly's Board of Publication negotiated for the purchase of all the private newspapers in the church and consolidated them into one paper, The Cumberland Presbyterian.

In 1879 Rev. J. H. Wofford began the publication of another paper, known as the Texas Observer, which was published at Tehuacana. Later it was issued as the organ of Trinity University under the editorship of Revs. E. B. Crisman and J. S. Groves. In 1887 Rev. W. B. Preston became editor. About that time the name was changed to the Texas Cumberland Presbyterian and it was moved to Dallas.

In 1886 or 1887 Rev. S. C. Lockett began the publication of a paper at Bertram, Burnet County. This paper was first called Our Little Helper, and was published bi-monthly, but soon it was enlarged and the name changed to Our Church Helper, and later to the Texas Church Helper. Rev. John Hudson and Rev. J. W. Pearson were at different times associated with Lockett in the publication of this paper, which was later moved to Hutto.

## HOME MISSIONS

Waco was taken under the care of the General Assembly's Board of Missions in 1875. At that time a church building had been erected at a cost of some ten thousand dollars on which there was an indebtedness of three thousand, which it was thought at the time was well provided for. Difficulties soon arose, however, due to the failure of the insurance company which held the notes. The board appointed Rev. W. G. L. Quaite to canvas for funds in the adjacent territory, but not until a period of five or six years had passed was the financial stress relieved so that the mission became self-sustaining. Missionaries who served under the direction of the board were Revs. E. J. Gillespie, R. J. Haynes, Alpha Young, and W. A. Hyde. The board contributed about one hundred dollars annually to the support of the missionary.

The church at McKinney was taken under the care of the board of 1876 and steps were taken to pay off the indebtedness on the church. Rev. W. G. L. Quaite served as the board's agent in accomplishing this task. Within two years $2,400 of the $4,500 debt had been paid, and the rest provided for. During this time the congregation employed and supported its own pastor.

In 1882 Rev. W. B. Preston was appointed as missionary to San Antonio. The plan of procedure adopted was first to raise a building fund and then inaugurate regular worship. Within a year a church building had been purchased and a small congregation gathered. By 1887 the congregation had been built up to 73 members. Rev. W. B. Preston then resigned and was succeeded by Rev. J. A. Francis.

Abilene and Colorado, in West Texas, were taken under the care of the board in 1885 and 1886. The work at Abilene was begun under the ministry of Rev. J. R. Hodges. In 1886 a congregation of 20 members and property worth $1,200 with $600 indebtedness was reported. Rev. A. J. Haynes had charge of this work for a time. It was decided to sell the original property and use the money to purchase a lot in a better location, which was done, leaving some $200 with which to start a building fund. This work was interrupted by the severe drouth of 1886. Rev. J. A. Robinson was in charge of the Colorado mission, which in 1886 and 1887 reported more than fifty members.

Tyler was selected as a mission point, and Rev. R. T. Phillips began his work there under the direction of the board in 1886. He devoted the first two years of his work largely to raising funds for building purposes. In 1888 a commodious brick building was completed, and by that time thirty members had been got together to be formed into an organization.

## WOMEN'S MISSIONARY WORK

Organized women's missionary work had its beginning during this period. There is a record of several local societies prior to the organization of the Woman's Board of Missions which took place at Evansville, Indiana, in 1880. There is a missionary society at Marshall which has been in continuous existence since 1875. In the Corsicana church on September 18, 1878, there was organized what was known as the Ladies' Relief Society. As implied in the name, and as set forth in the "Constitutional Rules," the society's object was to provide all possible relief to all in need of both material and spiritual things. Among the rules of the society the following have been noted under Article IV: (1) "Every member of the society is expected to lay by **each week one nickel** or more as God has prospered her." (2) "These amounts will be brought to the meetings of the society each month and deposited in a box provided by the Treasurer." Also under (6), "Any gentleman who is willing to pay $1.00 per month for the use of the society may be elected an **honorary member.**" On June 8, 1880, this society was reorganized under the care of the Woman's Board of Missions.

From a History of Corsicana Presbytery the following information was obtained: "In a diary of Mrs. E. E. Malloy, the first president of Corsicana Presbyterial Society, is written: 'This (Corsicana) presbyterial society was organized at this place September 15, 1887, at the fall session of what was then known as Kirkpatrick Presbytery; said society was organized by Mrs. S. E. Bucking who was at that time vice-president of what was then known as Brazos Synod.'" From this it is gathered that a synodic organization of the women's missionary work was maintained prior to that date. This was the period of beginnings for this work which was soon to be the means of accomplishing great things in the support of the foreign mission work, which has been largely committed to the Woman's Board of Missions.

### REVISING THE CONFESSION OF FAITH

During this period there was a growing demand throughout the church for a revision of the Confession of Faith by a restatement of its teachings in a form more nearly in accord with the accepted principles of Cumberland Presbyterianism. Heretofore the adopted creed of the church was simply the Westminster Confession modified by the elimination of certain sections in which the doctrines of unconditional election and reprobation were most boldly set forth, and the substitution of statements drawn up in accordance with the belief of Cumberland Presbyterians. But this did not suffice to eliminate all the objectionable features, for the deductions drawn from the principles on which the Westminster Confession was premised, permeated the whole book. It was a system, the objectionable features of which could not be eliminated simply by the changing of a few words, paragraphs, or even whole sections.

Of particular interest is the fact that the move by

which the revision was accomplished was launched by the General Assembly held at Austin in 1881, and in response to a memorial from Tehuacana Presbytery, within the bounds of which Trinity University was located. The chairman of the committee to whom this paper was referred was the Rev. A. Templeton, who was then pastor of the church at Corsicana. The committee recommended the appointment of a committee of three to revise the book, and a committee of five to review and revise the work of the first committee. Rev. S. G. Burney, Rev. A. Templeton, and Ruling Elder John Frizzell were appointed to constitute the first committee, to whom was given the responsible task of writing the book which would express the belief of the church.

The Confession of Faith as submitted to the next General Assembly, which met at Huntsville, Alabama, was adopted with but minor changes, most of them verbal, and sent down to the presbyteries for their approval. The vote of the presbyteries in favor of the new book was almost unanimous, and it became the constitutional law of the church.

Whether considered from the standpoint of its reasonable, Scriptural theology, or from that of its literary style, it is outstanding as a clear exponent of evangelical truth. It is indeed a work of art. The long, involved sentences "hard to be understood" which characterized the Westminster Confession were replaced by plain, simple statements that even a child can grasp. Moreover, in its teachings regarding the plan of salvation, the "via media" between the extremes of Calvinism on the one hand and Arminianism on the other has been pursued. It sets forth the fundamental truths upon which all successful evangelistic effort must be launched. This book, which has continued to be the recognized statement of Cumberland Presbyterian doctrine and polity until the present time, represents a distinct advance in the writing of church creeds.

This was Dr. Templeton's last great work. On June 28, 1882, just following the Huntsville Assembly, he departed this life.

### CHARACTERISTIC INCIDENTS—"SHOOTING UP" THE MEETING

Revs. B. E. Bowmer and E. D. Dysart were holding a revival meeting in 1889 in Coke County near where Bronte now stands. At the part of the service where mourners were being called, while a Methodist minister was praying and heaven and earth seemed almost to have come together, shooting was heard on the outside. The night before a doctor's dog had been hung to a tree and he had been hunting all day for the party who did it. Naturally it was thought when the shooting began that the two had come together. However, one of the brethren asked the people to keep quiet. They did, and there were several conversions. Later it was learned that those who did the shooting were only ruffians who were passing by and thought to break up the meeting.

### INCIDENTS IN THE LIFE OF REV. Y. H. HAMILTON

We have already referred to the Rev. Y. H. Hamilton's removal to Hill County soon after the close of the Civil War. In those days it often became necessary for men to take the law in their own hands and administer it accordingly. The country abounded in horse thieves, cattle thieves, murderers and drunkards, and the life of the preacher who preached against these things was always in danger. Rev. Y. H. Hamilton had, in the Woodbury community, the equivalent of a bodyguard in the person of two young men friends of his who attached themselves to him and would follow him to other "meeting houses" to see that no harm befell "Parson Hamilton." Several interesting incidents are told concerning this "body guard." On one occasion when Hamilton was engaged in a debate at Peoria with a minister of a heretical denomination, the other minister got to dealing too much in personalities, or at least these two young men thought so. After a consultation among themselves they decided it was time for them to go into action, so they mounted their mustangs, drew their six-shooters, rode up and down the aisles of the brush arbor where the debate was being staged and literally shot up the debate. They had no intention of hurting anyone, but were intent only on protecting "Parson Hamilton" from insult.

Hamilton had a close friend in the person of an aged Presbyterian minister. As he wore a long flowing beard, he was often referred to by the arrogant bullies of the community as "Moses." One day Hamilton's "bodyguard" came riding post haste to his farm two miles from the village of Woodbury to tell him that a certain bully had led Brother Blank over the village by his beard, and they wanted to know how to handle the situation. Hamilton evidently was a firm believer in righteous indignation, for this so enraged him that he took his black snake whip, mounted his horse, rode to the village and horse whipped the fellow within an inch of his life and ordered him from the community.

On another occasion Hamilton was conducting a protracted meeting in a log schoolhouse known as Friendship, and was being constantly annoyed by some very tough and mischievous young fellows who had vowed to break up the meeting. One night Hamilton dared them to come in and sit on the front seat and listen to him preach a sermon. They took the dare and no sooner had got seated than the preacher drew his six-shooter and held it on them until he had finished his sermon. As soon as he had finished he asked the congregation to stand and sing "Amazing Grace, How Sweet the Sound," and gave the invitation to the mourners bench. These young fellows were the first to come. They were converted and joined themselves to the others as a part of Parson Hamilton's bodyguard. In those days more ways than prayer were used to get people into the church. This kind of procedure might not receive the approval of some of our pacifist brethren today, but it worked in the times which produced men of the type of Y. H. Hamilton.

### BIOGRAPHICAL SKETCHES

While the church was extending its borders westward, there were many men who came into the older presbyteries who deserve mention for their work's sake. To mention a few of them will awaken memories.

**Rev. Ed Hudson** was born in Randolph County, Arkansas, in about the year 1833. He joined presbytery at the same time that his older brother, John Hudson, joined, October 5, 1854. He entered the Confederate

army early in the war, and was shot through the back
and had to go on crutches the remainder of his life.
Just after the war he established a school at Kemp,
Kaufman County, where Rev. R. O. Watkins was then
preaching, and for many years taught school and
preached at various places in Kaufman County. He was
the first pastor of the Cumberland Presbyterian Church
at Terrell, which was organized in 1875 and was the
first church to be established in the town. He died in
May, 1887, at his brother's home near Georgetown.

**Rev. John Miller** was born in Bradley County, Tennessee, September 6, 1848. He came to Texas in 1872,
and in 1876 joined Kirkpatrick (now Corsicana) Presbytery as a candidate for the ministry. Two years
later he was licensed to preach, and in 1879 was ordained to the full work of the ministry. Like many
other preachers in that day, he farmed during the week
for a living and preached on Sunday. He did not build
on other men's foundations, but went out as a missionary into new and unoccupied territory, held meetings,
and organized churches. He was the founder of the
Lone Oak congregation, in Navarro County, in which
community he lived many years. He died April 17,
1903.

**Rev. C. B. Hodges** was born in Kentucky, November
28, 1820; professed religion in 1842; was taken under
the care of Obion Presbytery as a candidate for the
ministry in 1844; and attended Bethel College (Tennessee) two years, and old Cumberland College at
Princeton, Kentucky, one year. In 1851, he moved to
Missouri and remained there and in the adjoining ter-
ritories until the close of the Civil War. He organized
the first Cumberland Presbyterian congregation ever

organized in Kansas, and also the first in Nebraska. He then moved to Texas and united first with Red Oak Presbytery, later moving into the bounds of Guthrie Presbytery where the remainder of his ministry was spent. He built churches at Whitesboro and Nocona, this being the first church building erected in the latter town. He died at Nocona in 1901.

**Rev. William Roach** was born in Pendleton District, South Carolina, February 28, 1791, but moved to Tennessee in his youth, where he shared in those pioneer days when that country was being opened up. He came under the influence of the great revival which was then sweeping that part of the country, and was converted under the ministry of the Cumberland Presbyterians. He was personally acquainted with Rev. Finis Ewing and others of the founders of this church, and attended as a visitor the first synod of this church held in Kentucky. In the early part of 1870, he moved with his family from Crittenden County, Kentucky, via the Ohio and the Mississippi to the mouth of Red River, and up Red River and the cypress lakes" to Jefferson, Texas, thence overland to Red River County, Texas. The remainder of his life was spent in Red River Presbytery, where he assisted in organizing several congregations and held several preaching appointments, among others, Mustang, Deport, and Shamrock. He died at his home near Halesboro, Red River County, in 1889.

**Rev. John H. Day** was born in Jefferson County, Tennessee, January 14, 1829, and came to Texas in 1882. After coming to Texas he served the following churches: Shamrock, Stone's Chapel, Rocky Ford, Shiloh, Woodland, and Halesboro. He organized the churches at Halesboro and Stone's Chapel. Nearly a thousand were converted under his preaching. He was one of the three ministers who perpetuated Red River Presbytery in 1906, the others being Revs. S. H. Baldridge and J. H. Hendrick. He died February 6, 1921, and was buried at Bethel, near Fulbright.

**Rev. John H. Hendrick** was born in Warren County, Kentucky, July 25, 1840. He was ordained by Logan Presbytery in 1865. After several years spent in the ministry in Illinois, he came to Texas in 1881 and became pastor of the church at Clarksville. He also held pastorates at Terrell, Longview, and Dallas. He died at Bowling Green, Kentucky, March 16, 1919.

**Rev. William Rice Hendrick** was born in Warren County, Kentucky, in 1833, and joined Logan Presbytery in early life. In 1881, he came to Texas and located in Red River County, serving as pastor of the Bogata church eight years. Other churches he served in Texas included Bethel, Newport, Plano, Richardson, and Lake Creek. In 1895 he became pastor of the Bagwell church, in Red River County, and was pastor there when he was called home, December, 1897. He was associated with Revs. Ben Fuller, J. H. Day, Charles Manton, S. M. Templeton, and others.

**Rev. Benjamin Spencer** was born near Jackson, Tennessee, April 4, 1826. He came to Texas in 1847, and the following year was received under the care of Red River Presbytery at Paris, Texas, as a candidate for the ministry. He was licensed October 20, 1848, at Hopewell camp ground, near Clarksville, and was ordained to the full work of the ministry by Marshall Presbytery at Pine Tree, January 7, 1852, the ministers participating being Revs. Solomon Awalt, G. A.

Flowers, G. S. Templeton, T. B. Wilson, S. R. Chadick, and S. W. Weaver. He was educated at Chapel Hill College, Daingerfield, and in later years Trinity University conferred on him the degree of Doctor of Divinity. During his active ministry he was pastor of churches at Bonham, Paris, Clarksville, Sherman, Terrell, Farmersville, Kemp, Groesbeck, Wortham, Garland, and other points. He gave a daughter, Miss Kate Spencer, to the mission field. She taught in the mission school at Aguascalientes, Mexico. He died February 2, 1905.

**Rev. William Bell Allen**, eldest son of Rev. and Mrs. W. M. Allen, was born in Pontotoc County, Mississippi, August 2, 1847. When about eight years old, he moved with his parents to Shelby County, Texas. He became a candidate for the ministry under the care of Marshall Presbytery in 1870 and was ordained in 1873 at Marshall. After several years spent as pastor at Pine Tree, Ewing Chapel, Atlanta, and other points, he was called to be the pastor of the church at Longview in 1883, which had just been organized with thirteen members. He remained here about twelve years, during which time a strong church was built up. He later established a mission at Shreveport, but in the struggle to establish that work his health was undermined. He was for thirty years stated clerk of Marshall Presbytery, and for ten years stated clerk of Texas Synod. He died at Marshall in 1930.

**Rev. Eddie Harrison Keasler** was born in Dickson County, Alabama, July 28, 1840; and entered the ministry at the age of twenty-one years, under the care of New Hope Presbytery. He came to Texas in 1872, locating in Cass County, and was a member of Marshall Presbytery from that time until his passing, August 2, 1913. At the time of his death, and for a good many years before, he lived at Marshall, where he had a long ministry with the churches at Hope Chapel, Fairview, Ewing Chapel, and Grand Cane, Louisiana. A grandson, Edwin A. Keasler, is now in Bethel College, at McKenzie, Tennessee, preparing himself to walk in his grandfather's footsteps.

**Rev. A. S. Hayter,** who came into Texas Presbytery in 1851, remained in Nacogdoches County until 1869 when he moved to Tarrant County, where Arlington now stands, and was one of the pioneer preachers in that section. He bought a section of land from one William Thomas, and as Thomas was out of the county when he came to close the trade, he gave a man by the name of Watson three thousand dollars in gold to give to Thomas and to tell him to get ready to move, as he (Hayter) was going back home and get ready to come to Tarrant County. He organized a church at Arlington in 1870 and taught the first school there. It is said that he used to preach two hours by his watch, but the last three and a half years condensed his sermons to forty minutes. He was the first county surveyor of Tarrant County, and was serving in that capacity when the Texas and Pacific Railroad came through in 1875, and assisted in directing the line through the most "peaceable" route. He once named a post office on his place as Haytersville, and later named the town of Arlington. He died in February, 1900.

### CONCLUDING REFLECTIONS

From the period of confusion arising out of the Civil War we have endeavored to follow the men and women of the Cumberland Presbyterian Church in Texas as they arose to the demands of the times to carry forward the work of preaching the gospel of Christ. We have portrayed the beginning and growth of a great educational institution; we have followed those pioneer spirits as they carried the gospel of Christ into the new settlements upon the advancing frontier.

An unusual interest was taken in building churches during this period. In the beginning there had been little need for giving much attention to the erection of buildings. The congregations, which were scattered sometimes over a whole county, came together only for their monthly services which usually began on Saturday at 11 o'clock, with services Saturday night, Sunday morning, and Sunday afternoon or night. The brush arbor or the log church or schoolhouse, materials for which had been hewn out of the forest, sufficed as a place of worship. In the towns there was usually one church in which all denominations were privileged to worship. With the growth of the towns, however, the situation was changed. The demands of the work necessitated the erection of commodious buildings and the employment of regular pastors.

There was an interest taken among the rural congregations in church building, also. In some presbyteries there was an organized effort along this line. In Little River Presbytery, which was mostly made up of rural churches, we note the appointment of a committee in 1883 to ascertain the amounts which could be raised for church buildings in the different congregations. The stated clerk of San Saba Presbytery, writing in the year 1899, states that when he came into the presbytery twelve years before there was only one completed church building in the presbytery; now there were seven.

The old time camp meetings on which the Cumberland Presbyterian Church thrived during its early history decreased in number as the country settled up and more elaborate church buildings were erected, though in a number of places they were continued for many years. Among the old camp meeting sites at which meetings were held regularly far up into this period may be mentioned Concord, Cherokee County; Rock Church, in Bosque County; and Mt. Zion, in Burnet County. Camp meetings were held in the latter community as late as 1897, and under the ministry of such men as Revs. R. B. Davis, S. C. Lockett, B. E. Bowmer, and John Hudson some wonderful meetings were held. In 1897 a camp meeting was held just following the meeting of Little Presbytery. During presbytery it was stated that the first meeting of that presbytery was held on the same ground forty years before, Revs John Hudson and W. R. Bauchman having been present at the time.

During this period the Cumberland Presbyterian Church was firmly planted in Texas. In 1888 there were in the state twenty-one presbyteries, and these had the oversight of hundreds of churches, many of which had already erected substantial buildings and employed regular pastors.

JUDGE F. H. PRENDERGAST

# Chapter IV

## THE CONSOLIDATED SYNOD

### (1888-1906)

IN RESPONSE to requests from the four synods of Brazos, Colorado, Texas, and Trinity, the General Assembly in 1888 provided for their consolidation into one synod to be known as the Synod of Texas. The first meeting of this consolidated synod was held, according to the order of the General Assembly, in the First Cumberland Presbyterian Church of Dallas, beginning Thursday before the third Sunday in September, 1888. Rev. R. O. Watkins, the first minister of any Protestant denomination ever to be ordained on Texas soil, who was now more than seventy years of age, being the appointed moderator, presided and preached the opening sermon.

Rev. J. W. Poindexter, D.D., of Guadalupe Presbytery, was elected moderator, and Rev. S. M. Templeton, of White Rock Presbytery, was elected stated clerk.

### HOME MISSIONS

When the consolidation of the synods was effected the mission stations in the bounds of the consolidated synod were San Antonio, Abilene, Tyler, and Texarkana.

Rev. J. A. Francis was the missionary at San Antonio, which was the oldest mission in Texas then under the care of the board. The old building having been condemned, there was need of a new building at once, and the churches of the synod were asked to raise two thousand dollars toward this work. The new building was soon afterward erected, and the San Antonio church

157

became self-sustaining. By 1906 there were three Cumberland Presbyterian churches in San Antonio.

An organization had been effected at Tyler with 29 members, and services were being held in their new house, under the leadership of Rev. R. T. Phillips, the missionary pastor. This church had grown by 1898 to 75 members. At that time Rev. W. J. Lackey took charge, and under his leadership the remaining debt on the building was paid off and the church greatly strengthened numerically and spiritually.

The work at Abilene was renewed in September, 1888, with Rev. D. C. DeWitt as missionary. Under his leadership the church was soon established and a new building erected.

Texarkana was adopted as a mission point in 1888. By 1890 a building had been erected and within three years had a membership of ninety, and property worth six thousand dollars. Rev. A. H. Whatley, and later Rev. W. B. Preston, served this church.

The work at Houston was commenced in 1893 under the leadership of Rev. J. M. Halsell, D.D., as a mission point under the care of Texas Synod. He went there without the promise of salary and commenced his work with seven members, all ladies. A lot was purchased at a cost of two thousand dollars and a chapel erected on the rear of the lot. This congregation enjoyed a substantial growth and developed into a strong church.

Prior to 1892 such mission work as was done, with the exception of that undertaken by the individual presbyteries, was under the direction of the Assembly's Board of Missions. Reports show that considerably more money was being expended in Texas by this board than was being contributed to it by the churches of

Texas Synod. In order to bring about a concerted synod-wide missionary program, there was organized in 1892 "The Missionary Association of the Synod of Texas of the Cumberland Presbyterian Church," its object being "the extension of Cumberland Presbyterian influence throughout the bounds of Texas Synod, through planting new churches and strengthening weak ones." Its membership consisted of "all persons by whom or for whom the sum of ten dollars shall be paid into the treasury of the association." The operations of the association were directed under the management of the executive committee, composed of five officers elected by the association, subject to the ratification of the synod. Revs. W. B. Preston, P. M. Riley, L. C. Collier, R. T. Phillips, and Charles Manton were the first officers. A membership of fifty-seven was enrolled before the adjournment of synod, and others were added later.

The receipts for the first year amounted to something over eight hundred dollars, and some effective work was done. Aid was rendered the Denison mission, and a synodic superintendent of missions was employed in the person of Rev. T. N. Williams.

The work of the association continued to grow, and on April 15, 1894, the first church to be erected under the leadership of the association was dedicated free of debt at Leonard. The association sponsored the erection of church houses in a number of other places, among them Temple and Taylor. The congregation at Temple was organized in December, 1893, with 18 members and worshiped under a board shed for several years until a more substantial building was erected.

This association was superseded about 1898 by the Board of Church Extension and Sunday School Work.

## WOMAN'S MISSIONARY WORK

An active woman's synodical misisonary organization was maintained throughout this period. The synodical vice-president of the Woman's Board at the time of the consolidation of the synods in 1888 was Mrs. S. L. Trumbull, of Sherman. At that time the Woman's Board of Missions had a vice-president in each synod to head up the work in the synod, instead of the synodical president as we now have.

Two Texas girls, Miss Mary Turner and Miss Kate Spencer, were sent as missionaries to Mexico during this period. The consecration of Miss Turner was the high point of the 1897 meeting of the Woman's synodic missionary society. She was stationed at Aguas Calientes, in the Mexican girls' school. Two years later the synodic society voted to undertake her support. A number of scholarships in the Mexican school were also sustained by the missionary societies. The Mexican work seems to have been the most popular field among Texas Cumberland Presbyterians at that time, on account of the fact that both Miss Turner and Miss Spencer were Texans.

## CHRISTIAN ENDEAVOR WORK

The Christian Endeavor societies during this time undertook the support of Rev. T. J. Preston, missionary to Japan. In the year closing September, 1899, $685.44 was contributed by the Christian Endeavor societies of Texas Synod to this cause.

SUNDAY SCHOOL WORK—THE ENCAMPMENT
MOVEMENT

The consolidated synod at its first meeting in 1888 elected a superintendent of Sunday school work in the person of Rev. G. O. Bachman, who served for two years in that capacity. He was succeeded by Rev. R. W. Lewis, who served three years under the direction of the newly elected Board of Sunday School Work. Under their leadership a new interest was taken along the line of improved methods of Sunday school work. Institutes were held in a number of the churches.

As early as 1888 a move was initiated for the establishing of a synodic Sunday school encampment. In 1890 there was a proposition before the synod to locate the encampment at Weatherford. The new Board of Sunday School Work, which was appointed at that time, was placed in charge of this encampment.

Accordingly, the board met with the Weatherford Park and Improvement Company and entered into a written agreement with them by which the use of a thirty-acre park was obtained for a period of twenty-five years. Provision was made for the publication of a small monthly paper in the interest of the encampment and the Sunday school work of the synod. This paper was called the Weatherford Chautauquan and was first conducted by Revs. R. W. Lewis and W. G. Templeton, and later by R. W. Lewis and W. B. Preston.

The daily fee for admission to the grounds was fixed at fifty cents, with season tickets at two dollars. Children five to fourteen years of age were admitted for half price. A membership plan was also established by which, for the sum of ten dollars, membership certificates were issued, entitling the holders to access to the grounds for five annual sessions of the encampment.

The first encampment was held July 1-8, 1891, and was a decided success. A well-arranged program was carried out. The attendance was considered good for the first year, and financially the encampment paid its way. Plans were made for the next encampment to be held July 30 to August 8, 1892.

The second encampment was not so successful from a financial standpoint, as an indebtedness of something over two hundred dollars was incurred. About this time the church lost its interest in the Weatherford park on account of the failure of the Weatherford Park Improvement Company. The synod made no provision to take care of the indebtedness incurred in the second encampment effort, and it devolved upon the members of the board to pay it, which they did, either out of their own pockets or from money raised by them as individuals for that purpose. Because of financial difficulties no effort was made to re-locate the encampment at that time. This board resigned in 1893.

The work done in this encampment consisted of courses of lectures by experts in various fields of Bible study and religious work, together with entertainment features. Dr. R. G. Pearson, an outstanding evangelist in the church at that time, was brought here for a series of Bible studies. The famous "Bill Arp" and "Sunshine Hawks" also appeared on the programs. The programs were under the direct supervision of Rev. R. W. Lewis, superintendent of Sunday school work in Texas Synod.

For several years no encampment was held. A permanent committee on Sunday school work was appointed in 1895, and the following year Rev. W. B. Allen was elected superintendent of Sunday school work in the synod. Under his leadership some constructive work was done by way of promoting Sunday school conventions in different parts of the synod.

The next encampment effort was at Glen Rose beginning in 1898. A resolution looking to the establishment of an encampment at Glen Rose was introduced in the 1897 meeting of synod by Rev. W. D. Wear, setting forth the fact that the citizens of Glen Rose, through a committee appointed for that purpose, had offered to donate five acres of ground, build a tabernacle 90 by 60 feet, fence the ground, and put an artesian well near the tabernacle provided Texas Synod would locate its encampment there. The resolution called for the appointment of a commission of seven to investigate the merits of this proposition and to accept it if in their judgment it was found to be the right thing to do. Rev. W. D. Wear was appointed chairman of the commission.

It was largely under his leadership, therefore, that the encampment was established at Glen Rose in 1898. It was known as the Glen Rose Assembly. Glen Rose was then becoming famous for its artesian wells of sulphur water. Assemblies were held there in 1898 and 1899, but on account of the distance from the railroad, it was decided to remove the Assembly to a more accessible location. It was moved, therefore, the following year to Waxahachie, where it was continued with increasing success under the name of the Waxahachie Summer Assembly and Chatauqua.

These encampments and assemblies were a forward step by way of affording normal instruction in Bible study, Sunday school work, and other phases of religious activity. An interesting feature of the Waxahachie Assembly was the erection of a facsimile model of the Old Log House in which the Cumberland Presbyterian Church was organized.

## NEW PRESBYTERIES

Two new presbyteries situated within the state of Texas, Pease River and Snyder, appear on the roll of Texas Synod during this period.

The building of the Fort Worth and Denver Railroad during the eighties opened up a vast territory in Northwest Texas, and true to its history in other places, the Cumberland Presbyterian Church was among the first to occupy the field. The pioneer Cumberland Presbyterian preacher in this section seems to have been Rev. W. D. Wear. In 1888 he organized a church at Vernon, which was at that time in the bounds of Gregory Presbytery. This soon developed into a strong congregation. He also organized churches in several other towns along the Fort Worth and Denver. Probably no preacher in Texas in his day organized more churches than Rev. W. D. Wear. He is said to have been an extraordinary preacher, possessed of unusual power. It is said that when he preached on such themes as "The Barren Fig Tree" and "The Judgment Day" the audiences would jump on the benches and the women pull their hair while crying to God for mercy.

By 1890 churches at Childress, Chillicothe, Harrold, Quanah, Seymour, and Vernon had been enrolled in Gregory Presbytery.

The order for the formation of Pease River Presbytery was passed by Texas Synod in September, 1890, from the record of which we quote as follows:

"That the Synod grant the prayer of the Gregory Presbytery, asking the formation of a new presbytery to be known as the Presbytery of Pease River of the Cumberland Presbyterian Church, with the following boundaries, viz.: Beginning at the south-east corner of Baylor County, thence west along county lines to north-west corner of Yoakum county, thence north with line between Texas and New Mexico to north-west corner of the Panhandle, thence east to north-east corner of the Pan-handle, thence south along the line between Texas and the Indian Territory to the north fork of Red River, thence down said river to north-east corner of Wilbarger county, thence south with east lines of Wilbarger and Baylor counties to place of beginning; including the following ministers, viz.: W. D. Wear, J. Phillips, J. A. Zinn, A. W. Rogers, Q. D. Elder, W. M. Speegle, and I. S. Davenport.

"That the first meeting of said new presbytery be held at Chillicothe, Hardeman county, beginning at 7:30 o'clock P. M., on Thursday before the first Sabbath in October, 1890. And that the Rev. W. D. Wear be the first Moderator, and the Rev. Q. D. Elder be his alternate."

From the above it will be seen that this presbytery originally included what was known as Greer County, which formerly had been considered a part of Texas, but is now a part of Oklahoma, the south fork of Red River having finally been designated as the boundary instead of the north fork. In 1891 a new presbytery known as Greer County was created, and several of the above named ministers, namely, Q. D. Elder, W. M. Speegle, and J. A. Zinn, fell in the bounds of the new presbytery.

Rev. A. W. Rodgers went to the Panhandle as a missionary before the new presbytery was organized. The eastern presbyteries were burdened for that vast western field and wanted to send a missionary, but had no funds. Rev. A. W. Rodgers said, "Send me." So with seventy-five dollars in cash and unwavering confidence in the promises of God, he took his wife and five children and located at Claud, Armstrong County. He organized churches at Amarillo, Canyon City, and several other places.

In 1890 Rev. W. M. Robison was endorsed by synod as an evangelist to the territory occupied by Pease River Presbytery which was then being organized. A few years later we find him located at Memphis where he led in the erection of a church house.

Among other ministers who helped to plant the Cumberland Presbyterian Church in that great western field were Revs. O. W. Carter, J. M. Burrow, and M. F. Karnes. Rev. O. W. Carter was for several years pastor of a group of churches including Canyon City, Tulia, and Silverton. Rev. J. M. Burrow took charge of the Amarillo church when it had only twenty-three members, and later preached at Canyon, also. Another of the early pastors of the Amarillo church was Rev. P. F. Johnson, who is known so well throughout the church for his services to Bethel College and the Cumberland Presbyterian Theological Seminary at McKenzie, Tennessee, from 1908 to 1925. He was pastor of the Amarillo church in 1895.

By 1906 every town of importance on the Fort Worth and Denver Railroad between Fort Worth and Amarillo had a Cumberland Presbyterian church.

On the western border of Abilene Presbytery the Cumberland Presbyterian Church was also keeping abreast with the advancing frontier. One of the first Cumberland Presbyterian preachers in the territory around Sweetwater was Rev. W. W. Werner. His location in the early nineties was Roby, in Fisher County.

In the spring of 1892 he wrote to a younger minister, Rev. J. L. Elliott, with whom he had worked in Johnson County, urging him to come west and take work in that section. He did so, and for a number of years made Sweetwater his home. As the churches in that sparsely settled and extremely drouthy country were small and hard pressed, he accepted an opportunity of learning the photographic business with which to supplement the meager salaries which his churches paid him. In connection with his photographic gallery he handled the only stock of Bibles, Testaments, and other religious books that was kept in the town of Sweetwater at the time. He organized churches at Dora, Roscoe, Union Chapel (later moved to Loraine), White Flat, and Mary Neal.

In 1904 Snyder Presbytery was formed, embracing Nolan, Fisher, and Stonewall Counties on the east and extending westward indefinitely. This new presbytery was directed to hold its first meeting at Snyder on Thursday before the second Sunday in November of that year. Rev. W. W. Werner was appointed to preside until the election of a moderator.

The names of a number of the presbyteries were changed during this period. Most of the presbyteries were originally named either for some river which was embraced in their bounds or for some one of the older preachers of the church. Now there was a tendency to change the name to that of one of the larger towns. In 1890 the name of Kirkpatrick Presbytery was changed to Corsicana, and White Rock was changed to Dallas. In 1895 the name of Buffalo Gap Presbytery was changed to Abilene. Parsons was changed to Weatherford in 1901; San Saba to Brownwood in 1902; Red

Oak to Fort Worth, and Pease River to Amarillo in 1903; and Guthrie Presbytery was changed to Denton in 1904.

Several consolidations of presbyteries were also effected. In 1901 Trinity Presbytery was consolidated with Texas Presbytery. In 1903 Little River and Colorado Presbyteries were consolidated to form Austin Presbytery, and in 1904 Tehuacana Presbytery was consolidated with Corsicana Presbytery.

## REMOVAL OF TRINITY UNIVERSITY

As early as 1888 there was agitation for the removal of Trinity University from Tehuacana to some larger town. The joint committee, in locating the school at Tehuacana, aimed not only at securing a healthful location, but at putting the institution where it would be away from the temptations and evil influences which were to be had in the city. Some felt, however, that the school would be more prosperous if located in some good town. There was a certain amount of dissatisfaction over the fact that over a period of several years there was a decrease in the number of students, which had been brought about largely by the increase in the number of colleges and the development of the public free school system.

The synod in 1888 passed measures which were designed to set at rest the question of moving the school, and so far as the records show, the question was not agitated again until 1899. At that time the million dollar endowment campaign was under way throughout the church. A resolution was introduced in the synod instructing the Board of Trustees of Trinity University in arranging the form of subscription for the endowment of that institution to omit any provision binding the endowment thus raised "to the present or any other location of the school."

In 1900 a number of memorials from various presbyteries were before the synod bearing upon the question of the removal of Trinity University, most of them favorable to the proposition. These were referred to the Committee on Overtures. The committee was hopelessly divided in its report. The majority of the committee brought in a report favoring outright the removal of school to a larger town, and calling for the appointment of a committee of seven to receive bids for the new location. One member submitted a report recommending the appointment of a committee to study the whole matter for a year and report back at next meeting of synod. The other remaining member submitted "that Trinity University is properly and judiciously located" and should remain where it is. By a vote of 53 to 44 the synod adopted the majority report.

The synod at its 1901 meeting selected Waxahachie to be the location of Trinity University. Meanwhile, there was much dissatisfaction among the people of Tehuacana over what was being done, and an injunction was threatened. Finally, however, through a conference with the people of Tehuacana a peaceful adjustment was worked out, by which the campus and buildings, together with the vacant lots at Tehuacana were turned back to a board selected by them, and they in turn agreed to the removal of all endowments belonging to the university.

On September 9, 1902, Trinity University opened its doors in its new location, with Rev. L. C. Kirkes as president.

## TEXAS FEMALE SEMINARY

Texas Female Seminary was established at Weatherford by the Synod of Texas in 1889, and opened its first session September 8, 1890, under the presidency of Rev. J. L. Dickens. For the many who proferred sending their daughters to a female school, this institution met a real need. It was located just south of the town of Weatherford on an elevation constituting the divide between the Brazos and Trinity Rivers. Buildings erected included the college building, a stone structure valued at $16,000, and a large frame building for a dormitory, which was valued at $7,500.

After the first year, Rev. J. L. Dickens was succeeded by Rev. W. B. Farr, who served as president one year. From 1892 to 1897, Rev. J. S. Howard was president. During these years the seminary enjoyed a slow but substantial growth. In 1897 Miss Emma E. McClure, of Fort Smith, Arkansas, was elected president. Her administration was a very successful one. By 1899 the enrollment of students reached 175, as compared with 63 three years earlier, and an addition of sixteen rooms was made to the dormitory to accommodate the increasing number of students. Miss McClure continued as president until 1903, when she was granted a leave of absence in order that she might take a much needed rest. Rev. George M. Oakley served as business manager and Mrs. Oakley as principal of the school during her absence. The following year she resigned the presidency of the school, and Prof. L. M. Logan became president. He was succeeded in 1905 by Prof. A. L. Groves, of Whitewright.

The seminary was begun with a considerable indebtedness which it was planned would be paid off from the sale of town lots adjacent to the school. There was a shrinkage of values, however, and the school was faced with difficulties, and several times was in danger of being lost to the church. In 1893, the indebtedness was reported to be thirteen thousand dollars, with seventy-five lots remaining unsold which were estimated to be worth two hundred dollars each. The synod appointed a special committee to devise plans to pay the debt, consisting of Revs. L. C. Collier, J. M. Martin, and R. W. Lewis, and through their efforts the debt was refinanced and reduced to $10,452.00. In May, 1894, Rev. J. H. Hendrick was appointed agent to solicit subscriptions to liquidate the debt, with the understanding that the subscriptions were to be payable when the whole amount was raised. He succeeded in obtaining subscriptions to the amount of several thousand dollars, but not enough to carry out the plan as proposed. In 1899 and 1900, Rev. W. B. Preston served as financial agent for the school in connection with his pastorate of the church in Oak Cliff, Dallas.

The school continued to be hindered by indebtedness, however, until the meeting of synod held at Weatherford in September, 1902. At that meeting the needs of the seminary were presented, and an offering amounting to $202.30 in cash for the immediate needs of the school had been made, when Rev. R. T. Phillips proposed to be one of thirty men to guarantee payment of the remaining indebtedness, which had by that time been reduced to about three thousand dollars. The required amount was raised by subscription and subsequently paid, and the school relieved of the burden of debt under which it had labored so long.

## THE SHEPPARD HOME

The plan of establishing a home for superannuated ministers and their families seems to have originated with Mrs. Tennie Sheppard, of Round Rock, and she and her husband, H. B. Sheppard, were the principal contributors to this enterprise. Texas Synod, at its meeting in 1902, took the matter in hand and appointed trustees to procure a charter for such an institution. Through the efforts of Rev. W. D. Wear, who served as financial agent for the board of trustees, donations to the amount of eleven thousand dollars in cash, real estate, and other valuable consideration were received, the largest donation being that of a six-room house in Round Rock. This was made the location of the home, and in 1903 the following trustees were named to have in charge the management of the home: Rev. John Hudson, R. M. Castleman, H. B. Sheppard, Henry Adkisson, and F. M. Hedrick. The home was opened for occupancy December 1, 1904, and served as a home for some of the worn-out and disabled ministers of our church.

## THE UNION QUESTION

In 1903 the General Assembly of the Cumberland Presbyterian Church made overtures for union with the Presbyterian Church, U. S. A. (the northern branch of the Presbyterian Church) for union, by the appointment of a committee on Fraternity and Union to confer with a like committee from the other church. The result was a recommendation to the next General Assembly for union with the Presbyterian Church, U. S. A., "on the doctrinal basis of the Confession of Faith of the Presbyterian Church in the United States of

America, as revised in 1903, and of its other doctrinal and ecclesiastical standards."

Although the move for union was hailed by the leaders in the movement as a "spontaneous" desire for union on the part of both churches, there was much opposition in the Cumberland Church from the beginning. Of the memorials before the General Assembly in 1903 on the question of union, while eight presbyteries expressed themselves as favoring union, nine presbyteries memorialized the Assembly against the proposal. When the question of submitting the proposed plan of union to the presbyteries was before the General Assembly in Dallas, Texas, in 1904, a bare two-thirds majority of members voting on the question was obtained, and in the vote of the presbyteries on the question, a bare majority of the presbyteries voted in favor of union. Unfortunately, at that time our Constitution permitted amendments being made upon the ratification of a majority of the presbyteries, each presbytery voting as a unit. As to the vote in the presbyteries, the tabulation showed that 691 ministers voted for "union" and that 470 ministers voted against it. Of the elders (the direct representatives of the people), 649 voted for, and 1,007 voted against the proposed "union." This made a total of 1,340 votes for "union" and 1,477 against, but these votes were so distributed that a majority of the presbyteries cast their votes for the proposed plan of union.

The opposition in the Cumberland Church was occasioned by the feeling that we would be giving everything and receiving nothing; that the proposed plan was not a union, but a merger of the Cumberland Presbyterian Church into a much larger denomination which

it was believed would not develop our institutions in the
same way that we were developing them, and would not
carry forward the work of evangelism among the common people as the Cumberland Church had done
throughout its history; that the "revision" of the Confession of Faith of the Presbyterian Church, U. S. A.,
did not revise, but that the system of theology against
which Cumberland Presbyterians had rebelled was still
there. Not a line had been changed. Two chapters, on
the subjects of the Holy Spirit and Missions, had been
added, and a Brief Statement proposing to interpret
certain chapters which were specially objectionable to
the Cumberlands did not actually change one word of
those chapters, and left untouched many other chapters in which the logical consequences of the system
were written.

Consequently, though the General Assembly, upon re-
ceipt of the returns from the presbyteries, declared
that the "union" had been carried, many Cumberland
Presbyterians resolved to perpetuate the Cumberland
Presbyterian Church. The returns from the presbyteries were received by the Assembly at Fresno, Cali-
fornia, in 1905, but another year was necessary to consummate the proposed union. This was finally done, according to the action of the General Assembly, in 1906,
at Decatur, Illinois. The majority of the General Assembly then voted to adjourn "sine die" as a separate
Assembly, but more than a hundred commissioners representing presbyteries which had sent them to this Assembly to perpetuate the Cumberland Presbyterian
Church, continued the meeting of the General Assembly and adopted the following, which had been entered
as a protest, as the grounds of their action:

"1. The Assembly is without power to declare the Cumberland Presbyterian Church as a separate organization at an end.

"2. That unionists have no power, nor right to declare that the Confession of Faith of the Presbyterian Church in the United States of America, as revised in 1903, and its other Doctrinal and Ecclesiastical Standards have been adopted by the Cumberland Presbyterian Church in accordance with its Constitution. And in the opinion of these Protestants such statement is not correct.

"3. Said unionists had no power to transfer the allegiance of the Ministers, Elders, Deacons and officers of particular churches, judicatories, Boards and Committees to another denomination of Christians, and make them amenable to another church creed and constitution.

"4. Said unionists had no power to direct the Presbyteries of the Cumberland Presbyterian Church to send commissioners to the General Assembly of the Presbyterian Church in the United States of America."

While many of those who went into the "union" felt that the General Assembly, the highest court of the church, had spoken and must be obeyed, those who remained Cumberland regarded the General Assembly as having exceeded its constitutional power, as there was no provision in our Constitution to permit the merging of our church into another. Furthermore, with the Cumberlands, the whole matter of religious liberty was involved. While it is true the ministers and elders had promised to "submit themselves to their brethren in the Lord assembled in the various church courts," this was not considered binding when it was sought to transfer their allegiance to a creed and Constitution to which they had not subscribed. On these grounds the 106 commissioners who perpetuated the General Assembly of the Cumberland Presbyterian Church at Decatur, backed by thousands back home, resolved to perpetuate the church of their choice that it might go forward in fulfilling its mission in the world.

In conclusion, let us call the roll of the commissioners representing Texas presbyteries who were enrolled in the continued session of the General Assembly at Decatur: Ministers—J. B. Wright, B. E. Bowmer, D. J. Moore, J. W. Reid, W. J. Rogers, W. M. Robinson, and J. L. Elliott. Elders—R. H. Schooler, W. L. Stewart, B. T. Price, J. R. Suite, William Clark, and W. W. Beall.

# Chapter V

## REBUILDING

### (1906-1936)

FOLLOWING the adjournment of the Decatur Assembly, with its declaration, on the one hand, that the Cumberland Presbyterian Church as a separate organization was no more, and, on the other, the determination of that formidable host who resolved to perpetuate the Cumberland Presbyterian Church, it was inevitable that the lines should be drawn, and a painful process it was. Old ties, which had been formed by association in a common cause over a long period of years, were disrupted. In some instances entire presbyteries were lost to the Cumberland Church. In most of the presbyteries there was division. Some two or three of our Texas presbyteries experienced the loss of only a very few of their ministers. In others, a bare quorum remained to perpetuate the presbytery. In some instances even this could not be obtained until the synod had time to make provision for the reorganization of the presbytery or else consolidate it with some other. The majority of the ministers who remained in the Cumberland Presbyteran Church in Texas were men past middle age—men who had spent their lives in building up the church and could not now get the consent of their own minds to join in a movement which they viewed as the tearing down of that which they had wrought hard to build.

When the various presbyteries met during the summer and fall, the question would immediately arise whether this presbytery is a presbytery of the Cumberland Presbyterian Church or of the Presbyterian Church, U.S.A. As an illustration of what happened in many of the presbyteries, we shall mention only one. Austin Presbytery met during the summer of 1906 at Shady Grove, in Burnet County. Upon the announcement that this presbytery was now a constituent part of the Presbyterian Church, U. S. A., Rev. John Hudson arose and asked all who were still Cumberland Presbyterians to follow him, whereupon the group who went with him retired to the schoolhouse near-by. It was found there were only two ordained ministers present, they being Revs. John Hudson and J. L. Stevenson. There not being a quorum present, the members adjourned to meet at the Sheppard Home at Round Rock, where, with Rev. Jesse Marshall, an inmate of the home, the presbytery was duly constituted, and a licentiate, W. G. Griffith, was ordained to the full work of the ministry and Austin Presbytery perpetuated.

Texas Synod had adjourned to meet at Abilene in September of that year. At the appointed time a quorum met and constituted the synod, electing Rev. J. W. Reid, of Gregory Presbytery, moderator, and Rev. S. C. Lockett, stated clerk. The synod then adjourned to meet in Dallas a few days later.

As was the case with most of the presbyteries, the few ministers who remained entered upon their task bravely, and set to work to rebuild upon the old foundations from which the superstructure had been swept away. A high point of the Dallas meeting was a conference of the forces presided over by Rev. W. M. Bunch, in which two hours were spent in carrying out a program previously arranged. Speeches were made by Judge F. H. Prendergast, Rev. J. H. Hendrick, D.D., and others, after which reports were heard from the field. More than two hundred people were present for this meeting.

An appeal from Dr. F. M. Proctor for aid in rebuilding the church at Bellevue, which had been destroyed during that year by a storm, was responded to by a free will offering.

Plans for synodic mission work, with a view of getting the loyal forces in working condition, were launched courageously. Although their church property was, for the most part, in the hands of the Presbyterian Church, U. S. A., and other discouragements had to be faced, the loyal Cumberland Presbyterian ministers and elders who made up that synod sounded no retreat.

A number of consolidations of presbyteries had to be effected during the period of reconstruction. The presbyteries of Abilene and Snyder were consolidated under the name of Sweetwater Presbytery at the 1906 meeting of synod. The presbyteries of Fort Worth and Weatherford were consolidated under the name of Weatherford Presbytery. During the following year, Dallas and Bonham Presbyteries were consolidated, and the larger part of the territory formerly occupied by Bacon Presbytery was added to this presbytery. The presbyteries of San Antonio and San Jacinto were left in a disorganized condition, and all of their congregations lost to the Cumberland Church. The territory of the former was added to Austin Presbytery, and that of the latter to Corsicana Presbyery. In 1910, Red River Presbytery was consolidated with Dallas-Bonham Presbytery, and Waco with Corsicana.

Greenville Presbytery, which was continued for several years with barely a quorum, was consolidated with Texas Presbytery in 1913.

Several pieces of church property were thrown into litigation by one side or the other within a short time after the "union" was declared to be in effect, and the outcome of these suits was awaited with much anxiety. When the Jefferson case, the first to reach the Supreme Court, was decided in favor of the Presbyterian Church, U. S. A., it was evident that the Cumberland Presbyterian Church had little to hope for by way of retaining its property rights in Texas. The Supreme Court refused to go behind the decision of the majority of the General Assembly, and in effect declared the General Assembly to be supreme court as well as legislative body, the sole interpreter of the constitutionality of its own acts. The Cumberland Presbyterians had no other recourse than to accept the inevitable loss of practically every piece of church property in Texas that was claimed by the Presbyterian Church, U. S. A. The Cumberlands had never had control of Trinity University and the Texas Female Seminary since 1906. The Sheppard Home was operated for several years by the two boards (Cumberland and Presbyterian, U. S. A.) acting jointly. This arrangement was continued until about the year 1911 when the property was sold by the Presbyterians, U. S. A.° All of the town and city churches, almost without exception, were occupied by the Presbyterian

---

*Mrs. Tennie Sheppard bequeathed to Texas Synod another home for old ministers, which became the property of the synod in 1911. This was subsequently sold and the proceeds placed in the hands of the trustees of synod.

Mrs. Ollie Glass
Baucom

Rev. J. H. Hendrick,
D.D.

Church, U. S. A.  A few small town and rural churches, where there were no members who went into the "U. S. A." church, remained permanently in the hands of the Cumberlands.  But, for the most part, the Cumberland Presbyterian Church was faced with the task of gathering its forces together and rebuilding from the ground up.

As to the losses sustained by the Cumberland Presbyterian Church as a result of the attempted union, it was estimated at the time that about two-thirds of the preachers, but perhaps not more than one-third of the membership, went into the Presbyterian Church, U. S. A.  Losses in membership to other denominations, as a result of the confusion attending the union disturbance and the lack of ministers to man the churches which might have been saved to the Cumberland cause, were almost as great as the number who went into the "union."  The percentage of loss, of both ministers and membership, was much greater in Texas than that of the church as a whole.  Very few ministers of middle age or younger were left in the Cumberland Church in Texas.  There was little property left to hold those who chose to "go whichever way the property went."  The fact that most of the ministers who were left were getting up in years, many of them very old, accounted for the necessity of consolidating presbyteries.  Those older ministers passed to their reward, or became unable to attend presbytery, before there was time for recruiting a new supply of young ministers to take their places.

The work of gathering together our forces which had been scattered and confused by the disturbances accompanying the attempted union was a tremendous task. The synodic mission work during those years was headed up by Revs. B. E. Bowmer and S. C. Lockett. They commenced their work as missionaries in Texas Synod under the direction of the General Assembly's Board of Missions immediately after the Decatur Assembly, and after synod met that fall they continued their work under the synodic board. In this capacity they traveled throughout the bounds of almost all of the presbyteries in the state, gathering together the scattered membership, perpetuating the various local congregations by the election of ruling elders where necessary, and endeavoring to bring them in touch with some minister who could supply them with preaching.

Among the presbyterial missionaries who were engaged in a similar work during this trying time, we find listed the names of Rev. J. L. Elliott, in Sweetwater Presbytery; Rev. J. B. Atkinson, in Brownwood Presbytery; Rev. J. D. Potts, first in Texas Presbytery and later in Austin Presbytery; Revs. F. M. Griffith and G. B. Russell, in Dallas-Bonham Presbytery; and Revs. M. F. Karnes and G. W. Crutcher, who did some work in Amarillo Presbytery prior to the reorganization of that presbytery in the fall of 1907. Rev. D. J. Moore also did a heroic work in Greenville Presbytery in holding together several congregations of that presbytery. These are some of the men who helped to perpetuate the Cumberland Presbyterian Church in Texas during the darkest hours of her history.

The First Cumberland Presbyterian Church of Dallas was perpetuated by a few loyal members who purchased property on Main and Hill Street, which was known as Cumberland Chapel, where the synod met in

1908. Cumberland Chapel was finally sold and property was purchased on the corner of Washington Avenue and Simpson Street, where a nice little frame church was built. The church being unable to meet its indebtedness on this property, it was posted to be sold at public auction when, in 1915, Rev. W. A. Boone, who was then secretary of the synodic board of missions, called on Rev. H. R. Allen, a young minister who had been reared near Dallas but had been away attending Bethel College, to take charge of this work. H. A. R. Horton, the well known writer of hymns and a loyal elder in this church, together with Rev. H. R. Allen signed the notes and took over the church, and as there were no missionary funds available, ran the church on faith for a while. Then the Woman's Board of Missions loaned the church some money, and soon the General Assembly's Board of Missions got behind the work, and in a few years this church was out of debt. Rev. H. R. Allen remained with this church for seven and a half years, during which time it was built up to a membership of around one hundred. Soon after his resignation, the First Church moved to its present location, Beacon and Ash Lane, where it has experienced a substantial growth.

The Cumberland Presbyterians in Fort Worth were gathered together and organized into a church by Rev. N. C. Pyles, of Mansfield, on October 4, 1908. This church was organized with eighteen members in a store house on the corner of Magnolia and Jennings Avenue. This church has worshiped in several locations and through the efforts of the faithful ones has continued its work, through difficulties, until the present time. Our church in Fort Worth has a great field.

In about the year 1913 the church property at Austin, which had been taken over by the Presbyterians, U. S. A., and sold by them to another denomination, was purchased by the Cumberland Presbyterians for the sum of twenty-three thousand dollars. Mr. R. M. Castleman, a ruling elder in that congregation, was the principal contributor. Thus the Austin church was re-established at its old location.

The hands of the brethren were greatly strengthened during the years just following the attempted union by the arrival of several strong preachers from other states who decided to make Texas their field of labor. Among them were Rev. W. A. Boone, who accepted the pastorate of the church at Marshall in the year 1907 and spent the remainder of his life in Marshall Presbytery, and Rev. I. V. Stine, who came to Texas in 1909, after a ministry of more than twenty years in Southwest Missouri. His first work in Texas was at Nocona and Mallard, in Montague County, and later he served the Decatur and Sunnydale congregations in connection with his field work for Cumberland College.

During this period the church had to devote its energies largely to rebuilding in those communities where our congregations had lost their property, and, consequently, little attention could be given to new fields, though some new fields were entered in the western part of the state, and a few new churches organized in other sections.

### NEW FIELDS—THE GARDEN CITY CHURCH

The Cumberland Presbyterian Church of Garden City, Glasscock County, was organized June 20, 1907, by Rev. J. B. Atkinson, who was at that time presbyterial missionary for Brownwood Presbytery. The charter members were Frank Miles, Mrs. S. E. Miles, Hattie Miles, J. T. Cox, Mrs. S. J. Cox, Essie Cox, S. R. Cox, Mrs. Mary Cox, Mary Cox, Doll Cox, Mrs. W. L. Lemmons, T. N. Beard, Mrs. Fannie Beard, Mrs. Mary Beard, and Mrs. S. A. Abernathy.

The new church building was dedicated July 5, 1908, by Rev. G. O. Hubbert, then of San Angelo. The elders at that time were Frank Miles, J. T. Beard, J. T. Cox, and W. F. Caulder. In the early days of this church and until his death, W. F. Caulder, a native of Scotland, was among its greatest benefactors.

Garden City was and is located thirty miles from a railroad, in the midst of a sparsely settled but prosperous ranch country. The church now has a membership of more than sixty, and has distinguished itself by its liberality, paying a salary of from forty to fifty dollars per month to their minister for one-fourth time, and having one of the largest benevolence budget apportionments of any church in Texas, which is always met in full.

A missionary society organized in the fall of 1929 by Rev. and Mrs. H. R. Allen has been active both in local and foreign missionary work. Besides their liberal offerings to missions, they have helped each year in some special way the orphans' home at Denton.

Among the oldest members of this church is Mrs. Mary Cox, known locally as Mother Cox. Through periods of discouragement which this church has experienced, isolated as it is and separated by many miles from other Cumberland Presbyterian churches, Mother Cox never gave up, and it is largely due to her efforts that an addition of four Sunday school rooms was made to the building in recent years. She and her husband, S. R. Cox, have seventeen descendants now members of the Cumberland Presbyterian Church.

## CHURCHES ON THE SOUTH PLAINS

After the union disturbance had taken its toll, the only remaining member of Amarillo Presbytery was Rev. O. W. Carter, who had by that time moved to Portales, New Mexico. Several congregations, or remnants of congregations, were still loyal to the Cumberland Presbyterian Church, but not a single piece of church property remained in the possession of the Cumberlands. Rev. O. W. Carter appealed to synod to take steps to reorganize the presbytery. This was done by the appointment of Revs. J. W. Reid and S. C. Lockett as a commission to reorganize Amarillo Presbytery. Rev. S. C. Lockett was unable to be present at the reorganization, but Rev. J. W. Reid called together the brethren of the ministry (some of whom had moved into the bounds of Amarillo Presbytery) and representatives of congregations that could be found, and November 8, 1907, at Memphis, Texas, the reorganization of Amarillo Presbytery was accomplished by transferring the name of Rev. C. N. Jarrell of Denton Presbytery and receiving the letters of Revs. B. H. Baker and C. W. C. Norwood, which gave the presbytery four ordained ministers. Rev. O. W. Carter was elected moderator and Rev. C. W. C. Norwood stated clerk.

Rev. T. M. Torbett was employed as missionary for this presbytery and in the early part of 1908 he visited several points on the South Plains and organized a church at Floydada. Among the charter members of this church was E. C. King, a son of Rev. Robert A. King who spent a ministry of forty years in northeastern Arkansas and southeastern Missouri. In his declining years he, too, made Floydada his home and died there November 4, 1914.

Meanwhile other ministers were becoming interested in the opportunities offered by the great South Plains region which was being opened up for farming, several of the larger cattle ranches having been cut up and offered for sale in tracts of suitable size. Rev. J. L. Elliott, a member of Sweetwater Presbytery, who was living at that time in Mitchell County, had organized a small congregation at Young's schoolhouse, near where the town of Wilson now stands, which was on or near the north line of that presbytery, and another at Slide, or Block 20, ten miles further west. These groups of Cumberland Presbyterians had been discovered by Rev. W. W. Werner who in the meantime had gone into the Presbyterian Church, U. S. A.

In July, 1908, a meeting of Sweetwater Presbytery was held at Young's schoolhouse. The members of Amarillo Presbytery were invited to attend, and some of them did. According to a plan suggested by Rev. J. L. Elliott, a concerted evangelistic campaign was adopted to be put into effect immediately after the adjournment of the presbytery. The ministers present were to go "two and two" to certain designated points and hold revival meetings with a view, in some instances at least, of organizing churches. One of these revival parties was composed of Revs. B. H. Baker and C. W. C. Norwood, the latter being a gifted evangelistic singer. After a few days' services at Block 20, they went to Lubbock where on August 8, 1908, in the home of E. P.

Earhart, the Lubbock Cumberland Presbyterian Church was organized with seven members.

Rev. J. L. Elliott was called to the pastorate of the Lubbock church, preaching there two Sundays a month and coming from his home near Loraine more than a hundred miles away. Services were held on Sunday afternoons in the Christian church. The following year Rev. J. L. Elliott moved to Lubbock and a church building was erected in which the first service was held on September 5, 1909, the congregation being seated on nail kegs and planks placed on boxes.

Rev. J. L. Elliott then preached on a regular circuit which included Floydada, Cone, Emma, and Petersburg on one trip, and Young's schoolhouse and Block 20 on another, his principal means of transportation during this time being a bicycle. During this time he organized churches at Emma and Petersburg, and after the town of Ralls was established he organized a congregation there which was largely made up of members of the earlier organization at Emma. During his five years' pastorate at Lubbock approximately one hundred members were received into the church, and Lubbock became one of the strongest churches in Amarillo Presbytery.

No history of the Lubbock church would be complete without mention of E. P. Earhart and his wife, Mrs. Eliza Earhart. Mr. Earhart was a product of the frontier, a true pioneer who had inherited those qualities of honesty and integrity characteristic of the West Texas cow man, but, although he had been a member of the church many years, he had not taken a very active part in the public services prior to the organization of the Lubbock church. He used to tell how during the time when Rev. J. L. Elliott was his pastor, he slipped out of prayer meeting one night and went home after his wife's overshoes, as a cloud was coming up, because, he said, "I saw that if I stayed there Brother Elliott was going to call on me to pray." He added, "And it didn't rain a bit." He soon overcame this reserve, and became one of the spiritual leaders of his congregation, as well as one of its greatest benefactors. He donated the first manse outright, and was one of the most liberal contributors in the building of both the old and new church buildings. He also assumed a large share in the financing of his church locally and abroad, and served frequently as moderator of his presbytery and once as moderator of the West Texas-New Mexico Synod.

Several other churches have since been organized in this region which are now doing good work. The most of the churches in Amarillo Presbytery now are on the South Plains, in a territory which was practically untouched by our church before the union disturbance. That is a large missionary territory for the Cumberland Presbyterian Church. In almost any town or community where one may go he will find one or more families of Cumberland Presbyterians, some of whom have been out of reach of the church of their choice for years. In one congregation organized a few years ago was a man who had not lived where there was a Cumberland Presbyterian church for twenty-seven years.

Among the ministers who have had much to do with the progress of the church on the plains we would mention Rev. A. A. Collins, who came out from Oklahoma in 1918 to be pastor of the Lubbock church and later was pastor at Floydada and other points; Rev. O. N.

DENTON C. P. CHURCH, ERECTED 1933

❖ ● ● ● ❖

REV. J. L. ELLIOTT
Pastor of Denton
C. P. Church

Baucom under whose ministry the new church building at Lubbock was completed in 1928, and Rev. O. A. Mealor, who passed to his reward while serving as pastor of the Olton church. Several other ministers who gave themselves to the work on the "plains" have met what seemed to be untimely deaths; among them, Revs. G. O. Hubbert and John F. Baker, each of them died while serving as pastor of the Lubbock church, and Rev. G. P. Humphries, who died at Floydada in the spring of 1928.

## CUMBERLAND COLLEGE

By 1910 all hope of regaining control of Trinity University and Texas Female Seminary was practically gone. At its meeting held at Olney in October of that year, Texas Synod appointed a committee to take under consideration the matter of establishing a college, survey the field, investigate resources, and report at the next meeting of synod. This committee consisted of Revs. B. E. Bowmer, J. W. Pearson, W. J. Walker, and Elders J. A. Smith and F. E. Allen.

Before the time for the next regular meeting of synod, an option was secured on a piece of property located in the town of Leonard, which had formerly been used for school purposes and which it was proposed to turn over to the synod upon the assumption of the indebtedness amounting to about seven thousand dollars. This property consisted of a three story brick building containing twelve rooms, and a two story dormitory for girls, containing thirteen rooms, situated on a campus of eight acres overlooking the town, which property was estimated to be worth about twenty-eight thousand dollars. A special meeting of synod was called to consider the proposition, and on

June 29, 1911, this property was purchased from the citizens of Leonard and Cumberland College was formally established, trustees elected, and arrangements made to procure a charter.

The college was opened September 12, 1911, with an enrollment of sixteen pupils, and experienced a substantial growth during the first session. By the end of the first year the enrollment in all departments had reached sixty-three.

The original board of trustees consisted of Rev. J. W. Pearson, president; Joe F. Hall, secretary-treasurer; John W. Groves; W. W. Witcher; and B. B. Braley. The faculty for the year 1911-12 consisted of Rev. J. W. Pearson, president and professor of Greek and Philosophy; DeCosta Howard Dodson, professor of Mathematics; John F. Baker, teacher of telegraphy; Diana Clarissa Miles, tutor of English; May Belle Manning, teacher of art; Gladys Marie Everett, director of music. Because of the increasing enrollment it became necessary to add another teacher at the beginning of the spring term, so Rev. W. J. Lackey was employed as dean of the theological department and business manager of the college.

The college had been launched with no endowment or financial resources of any kind, so it became necessary for the synod to make arrangements to meet the obligation incurred in the purchase of the college property. At the regular meeting of synod held at Richardson in the fall of 1911, plans were launched to obtain the needed funds by donation. At the same meeting, the trustees of Texas Synod were authorized to lend to Cumberland College the Sheppard bequest amounting to six thousand dollars. This loan was made for a term of three years, and secured by a deed of trust on the college property. By the use of this fund together with outside donations the original debt on the college property was paid off.

In the spring the prospects for attendance for the coming year looked so bright that the board felt justified in taking a forward step. George Medders of the Wichita High School was elected professor of science and English, and Mrs. George Medders teacher of domestic science. Revs. W. J. Lackey and J. W. Pearson took the field and canvassed for students during the summer. Rooms were completed for the library and scientific department, electric lights installed throughout the entire building, and other improvements made. A primary department was opened as an experiment, with Miss Maud Lackey in charge.

The bright prospects for the second year's opening, however, failed to materialize. The board's report to synod in the fall of 1912 showed only twenty-two students enrolled in the literary department up until that time. The income was found insufficient to meet running expenses.

The report to synod the following year showed financial difficulties still hindering, and an evident lack of support from the church at large. Still further deficits had been incurred. No interest had been paid on the fund loaned from the Sheppard estate. A committee consisting of Revs. W. A. Boone, I. V. Stine, and J. L. Stevenson was appointed to visit the school, ascertain the true conditions, and report to the members of the synod. The report of this committee as recorded in the synodic minutes of 1914 states that the school was found to be in excellent condition as far as its internal workings were concerned. Ten young ministers and one missionary student were enrolled. The General Assembly had put this school on a par with Bethel College in so far as the ministerial aid funds of the Board of Education were concerned. The total indebtedness, including the interest past due on four thousand dollars of the Sheppard estate funds (the interest on two thousand having been donated by order of synod, as that amount was given for educational purposes) was found to be about four thousand six hundred dollars, besides the principal of the Sheppard estate.

Meanwhile Rev. W. A. Boone was elected president of the college and teacher of theology. He was paid fifty dollars per month by the Assembly's Board for his services as instructor in theology. The report for 1915 lists the following as members of the faculty: Rev. W. A. Boone, president and teacher of theology; Rev. J. W. Pearson, languages; Rev. J. G. Willis, mathematics; Miss Della Campbell; and Prof. W. P. McAdow, music. By this time a considerable indebtedness had been created, including money borrowed from banks and obligations to former teachers. There was opposition to continuing the school. The synod, through its committee on education, recommended putting a man in the field to raise money to pay off the indebtedness.

In the spring of 1916 Rev. I. V. Stine was employed and entered upon his duties as financial agent for the school. He traveled over a large territory, and within five months, up to and including August, 1916, had collected $241.21 in cash over and above his salary and expenses, and notes in the amount of $7,829.50. These notes were for a period of ten years payable one-tenth each year. He continued in this work with increasing success until his death which occurred in May, 1917. It is believed by many that had he lived the school could have been pulled out of debt.

As it was, however, his work was not continued. The World War came on, the patronage on the part of the church was withheld, the banks brought suit for the amounts which had been borrowed from them, and on December 28, 1917, at a called meeting held in Dallas, the synod ordered that the school be closed on January 8, 1918. In the final settlement the property was sold, and after settlement of the debts contracted in opening the school and the amount due the banks, only about $250.00 was left to be returned to the Board of Trustees of Texas Synod in place of the six thousand dollars of the Sheppard estate which had been loaned to the college. Thus ended the somewhat tragic history of Cumberland College.

Even though it ended in failure so far as becoming a permanent institution was concerned, Cumberland College did serve a useful purpose during the few years it was in operation. Several of the young ministers of Texas and Oklahoma obtained valuable training here who otherwise would have found it impossible to attend school under Cumberland Presbyterian auspices. Among the ministers who are now active in our church who received at least a part of their training in Cumberland College are Revs. O. N. Baucom, R. E. Matlock, W. A. Bearden, G. L. Waddle, and J. S. Eustis. Among those who have passed on from labor to reward are Revs. John F. Baker, J. P. Herman, and A. E. Laine.

## WEST TEXAS-NEW MEXICO SYNOD

In 1915, a new synod was formed, composed of the presbyteries of Amarillo, Brownwood, Roswell (New Mexico), and Sweetwater, known as the Synod of West Texas-New Mexico. This synod held its first meeting at Lubbock, beginning September 15, 1915. Rev. J. L. Elliott, who was one of the leaders in the movement for the formation of this synod, served as its stated clerk throughout the four years of its existence. This synod held only four meetings. At the time appointed for the fifth meeting a quorum was not present, so the members present resolved themselves into a convention which petitioned the General Assembly to consolidate this synod with Texas Synod. The short life of this synod was due in large measure to the severe drouth of 1917-18 which wrought havoc throughout the West. Many of the churches were broken up through the removal of their members, and several of the preachers left. None of the four presbyteries were strong, numerically, to begin with. This synod never had a large attendance, but did some good work during the brief period of its existence.

At the meeting of Texas Synod held at Bogata in 1920, the meeting after the consolidation, the territory of Roswell Presbytery was added to Amarillo Presbytery, and Sweetwater Presbytery was divided between the presbyteries of Amarillo and Weatherford.

## WOMEN'S MISSIONARY WORK

In the Twenty-Seventh Annual Convention of Cumberland Presbyterian women which met in Dickson, Tennessee, in May, 1907, there were two Texas women in attendance who were to figure prominently in perpetuating the woman's missionary work of the Cumberland Presbyterian Church in Texas. They were Mrs. C. W. McKinney, of Dallas, who was the first synodic president after the attempted union, and Miss Ollie E. Glass, of Hughes Springs.

Miss Ollie Glass, daughter of Rev. and Mrs. W. S. Glass, was a Christian and a member of the Cumberland Presbyterian Church from early childhood, and gave her life to good works. In addition to the many posts of service which she occupied in her own church, she organized the W.C.T.U. in her town and served as its president. In March, 1910, she began her work as state organizer for the Texas Woman's Synodical Society, and while engaged in that work she organized many of the missionary societies which are living today. Later she was married to Rev. O. N. Baucom, a young minister who had cast his lot in Texas soon after the union disturbance. She was actively connected with the state work until her death, which occurred December 26, 1919. Rev. W. A. Boone said of her: "She has done more piecing together the fragments in the saving of the Cumberland Presbyterian Church in Texas than any other one person." In memory of her faithful, unselfish service, the Texas Woman's Synodical Society placed memorial windows in the San Francisco and Canton mission buildings.

The woman's missionary work has become well organized in all of the presbyteries in Texas, and has been a vital force in the rebuilding and expansion of the work of our church throughout the state. Several missionaries have gone out from Texas to the various mission fields under the direction of the Woman's Board of Missions, and a number of others are preparing for mission work. It was here that Miss Julia McCaslin answered the call to her life's work in the San Francisco Chinese mission. Miss Lois Hornbeak, of Corsicana, also taught in that mission for a time. In 1931, Rev. Davis O. Bryson, who was reared in the Shiloh community, Ellis County, responded, with his wife, to an emergency call which demanded workers to be sent at once, and went to Colombia, South America. Rev. and Mrs. Bryson are now at home on furlough after four years spent in that field. In 1932, Miss Betty Smith, of the Fort Worth church, was sent to the Colombia field as a missionary.

## HOME MISSIONS SINCE 1920

In recent years, a start has been made toward re-establishing the Cumberland Presbyterian Church in several Texas cities, namely, San Antonio, Wichita Falls, Amarillo, Denton, and Longview. Most of these had their beginning as presbyterial mission projects, though in severral instances the General Assembly's Board of Missions later came to their rescue. A number of other churches have been organized in smaller towns and rural communities, some of these through presbyterial missionary efforts, but in more instances through individual effort on the part of some minister who became interested to the extent of entering the field on his own initiative and without the promise of salary. Some of our best churches which have had their origin in this period were never under the care of any mission board.

During the synodic year of 1925-26, Revs. B. E. Bowmer and A. J. Mann were in the field as synodic missionaries and did a good work in the formation of several pastorates and the reviving of a number of congregations. They retired from the work after one year. All of the various plans for synod-wide mission work which have been advanced within the last few years have fallen down because of lack of support. This has been due in part to the many local situations demanding attention. There is no doubt, however, that the church in Texas has suffered through the lack of a concerted program of home missions.

### THE SAN ANTONIO CHURCH

In about the year 1920, Miss Dessie Gibbins, a young Texas woman who had been working in Washington, D. C., during the World War, came to San Antonio to work. Being a Cumberland Presbyterian and not having a church of her choice in the city, she became much concerned about establishing a church in San Antonio. One day in reading her church paper she came across the name of P. D. Starr, of San Antonio, Texas, in a list of donations to the educational endowment fund which was being raised at that time. A man who would make a contribution to the educational interests of the church such as he had made, she thought, would surely be interested in establishing a church in San Antonio. Very soon she got in touch with Mr. Starr and found that he, too, would be interested in having a Cumberland Presbyterian church in San Antonio, although the possibility of it had not occurred to him before. A few other Cumberland Presbyterians were found, and soon a ladies' missionary society was organized. An appeal was made to Austin Presbytery to send a minister to look over the field with a view of organizing a church. The presby tery sent its missionary, Rev. J. S. Eustis, and on August 20, 1922, he organized the First Cumberland Presbyterian Church of San Antonio with thirteen charter members. He preached once a month to the little congregation for a while.

On March 1, 1924, Rev. Hugh Watson took charge as the first regular pastor, holding services in the Y.M.C.A. hall. After a little more than a year, he resigned on account of ill health. About this time a small frame building was erected on a lot which had been purchased on the corner of West Elsmere Place and Aganier. Rev. J. R. Haws was then called as pastor and served four years, during which time there was a substantial increase in membersh'p, and the debt on the church property paid. In September, 1929, Rev. T. J. Tanner became pastor. Under his leadership the church has enjoyed a substantial growth, and is well organized in all of its departments; the frame building has been moved to the rear of the lot and an adjacent lot purchased with a view of erecting a new building; and the church has grown to be an increasingly vital factor in the religious life of the community in which it is located. The latest report shows a resident membership of 105, and the congregation, which has been aided by the General Assembly's Board of Missions from the time when its first regular pastor was secured, has voluntarily reduced the amount of aid received as the work has progressed. This church bids fair to become one of our strongest churches in Texas, for its members are ardent workers and strong in the faith.

## OAK CLIFF, DALLAS

This church had its beginning in a group of Cumberland Presbyterians, several of whom had been members of the Oak Cliff church (later known as Trinity Church) which was organized by Rev. D. G. Malloy in 1891. When that congregation went into the Presbyterian Church, U. S. A., the few members who chose to remain Cumberland joined in with other loyal Cumberland Presbyterians of Dallas in perpetuating the First Church. Among these were the family of Dr. M. D. Hudson (Dr. Hudson having died previous to this time), Prof. J. E. Rodgers, and Miss Mary Park. Professor Rodgers and Dr. Hudson were among the original elders of this congregation.

In 1922, when the First Church decided to build farther east in East Dallas rather than to build a down town church, Rev. H. R. Allen, according to his agreement with these members that if a down-town church were not built he would organize a church in Oak Cliff, organized the Oak Cliff church in an old store building at 328 West Seventh Street. From here the newly organized congregation moved a month later to the Rialto Theater, which was tendered for Sunday school and 11 o'clock services. It was soon decided to try to buy a lot, which was contracted for, and the building commenced at the present location, 300 West Eighth Street. Before the building was finished a revival meeting was held which greatly strengthened the church. The work grew rapidly for a time, and realizing the need of more room, plans were made for a basement. Beginning on the first Monday in September, 1925, being Labor Day, six hundred cubic yards of dirt and rock was removed with volunteer labor, and a basement built. In May, 1928, Rev. H. R. Allen resigned as pastor. Subsequently, due to reverses, financial and otherwise, the church was closed on or about January 1, 1932, and on April 4 was sold for the debt. Rev. H. R. Allen bought the property and came back to Oak Cliff to re-establish the church, starting with only fifteen members. The church has been turned back to the local trustees, and the note on the property refinanced, and every department of the church is now functioning. Oak Cliff is itself a city of 130,000 souls, and a great field for the Cumberland Presbyterian Church.

## OTHER MISSION POINTS

In February, 1930, a Cumberland Presbyterian church was organized in Wichita Falls with nine members. This congregation was organized by Rev. B. L. Baits, a minister living in the town, who has been its pastor ever since. Two of the charter members, Mr. and Mrs. Cull McDonald, had also been charter members of the San Antonio church. Here, as in the case of San Antonio, a ladies' missionary society had been established before the church was organized. This church located in a suburban district, where a congregation of fifty resident members has been built up.

The Amarillo mission was projected by Amarillo Presbytery, and the work was initiated largely through the efforts of Rev. O. N. Baucom. In March, 1934, the presbyterial board of missions appointed Rev. W. H. Cheatham, a young preacher from Tennessee who became interested in the work in the West, to take charge of the work of establishing a church in Amarillo, and on the fourth Sunday in April he met with five members at the court house and organized them into a church. In July, a revival meeting was held which resulted in four professions and nine additions to the church. Meanwhile, property was purchased in

ELMIRA CHAPEL, NEAR LONGVIEW, TEXAS, ORGANIZED 1896

OLNEY C. P. CHURCH, ERECTED 1926

CHURCH, MANSE, AND EDUCATIONAL BUILDING, ERECTED 1932-35

LUBBOCK C. P. CHURCH, ERECTED 1928

a growing residential section of the city, consisting
of two lots, on one of which was a seven-room house.
A part of this building was converted into a chapel.
Services were held one Sunday per month until November, when Rev. W. H. Cheatham moved on the field
to devote half time to this work. This arrangement
was continued until the summer of 1935, when he resigned. Since February, 1936, Rev. B. C. Welch has
had charge of this mission, which promises success.

In the spring of 1935, Rev. S. Q. Proctor was employed by the presbyterial board of missions of Mc-
Adow Presbytery as missionary for that presbytery.
In the course of his work he made a survey of the pos-
sibilities for organizing a church in Longview, where
there were a number of Cumberland Presbyterians,
and it was decided to establish a church there. The
congregation was organized in June, 1935, with seven
members, one of whom was not able to attend services.
A lot was purchased and a church erected at a cost of
about seven thousand dollars, the indebtedness on
which is rapidly being retired. As the result of a
revival meeting held recently, the membership has
been increased to nineteen.

### THE TEXAS ENCAMPMENT

In the summer of 1926 Rev. H. R. Allen conducted
an encampment under the auspices of Weatherford
Presbytery at Lover's Retreat, in Palo Pinto County,
which was attended by twenty-three persons, Rev. and
Mrs. W. H. McLeskey being present as speakers. The
following year a somewhat larger group met at Ovilla,
near the Shiloh (Ellis County) church. The third year
the Synod of Texas took over the encampment work
and a second encampment was held at Ovilla. At this

time, Rev. Clark Williamson, who had been elected General Secretary of Young People's Work for the Cumberland Presbyterian Church the year before, was present and rendered valuable service. At the close of this encampment, a conference of ministers and elders present was held in which recommendations to synod were outlined for the enlargement of the work. At the meeting of Texas Synod held at Dawson in October, 1928, the following was adopted:

"Sixth, we recommend that the time of the encampment be August 26-30, 1929, and the place be left to a committee composed of the following: Rev. J. L. Elliott, Rev. T. J. Tanner, Rev. Thomas H. Campbell, F. P. Arterburn, and Elders A. H. Smith and S. S. Bowmer.

"Said committee shall have charge of the arrangements for the work of the encampment, including the program and any other things that may be necessary to make the same a success.

"Seventh, we recommend that Rev. Clark Williamson be asked to direct the work of the program and that in preparing the same he be given a chance to suggest what is needed.

"Eighth, we recommend that a fee of 25 cents per person be charged for an investment certificate, and that this certificate be sold to as many as will buy, whether they come to the encampment or not. That the expense left unpaid from last encampment be paid out of this fund, and the expenses of the 1929 encampment be paid as far as possible out of this fund."[*]

Joe Wheeler Park, near Decatur, was the place chosen for the 1929 encampment, and plans were made for a full week of worship, instruction, and recreation. Courses of study taken from the Standard Leadership

[*]From report of Committee on Sunday School and Young People's Work.

Training Course which had recently been adopted by the Board of Young Peoples Work, were introduced into the Texas encampment for the first time. This encampment succeeded beyond all expectations, and fifty-one certificates of credit were issued.

The encampment committee was subsequently constituted by synod as the Board of Sunday School and Young People's Work, under whose direction the encampment work has continued with increasing success. The records show that there has been a substantial growth in attendance each year, with the exception of one year when the encampment was postponed on account of failure to obtain the needed equipment. In 1935, there was a registered attendance of 376 persons, of whom approximately 250 were camped on the ground for the full week. 149 certificates of credit were issued.

The encampment was established primarily for the young people, but a number of older people attend, many of whom enter into regular class work. The attendance has also included a large proportion of the active ministers of the synod. Conferences of ministers and laymen are held during the afternoon while the young people are observing study hours.

The encampment has proved to be one of the greatest unifying agencies of anything that has been attempted by Texas Synod in recent years, as so many phases of the church work are represented here. Its influence has been reflected in a marked increase in the attendance at the meetings of synod, and a growing interest in the work throughout the state. Many young people who have consecrated their lives here are going out to render service for Christ and the church.

Oak Cliff Cumberland Presbyterian Church

Headquarters of Texas Synodic Centennial Commission

It is worthy of note that a class in Cumberland Presbyterian Doctrine has been conducted each year, and almost without exception this has been the largest class in the encampment, which proves that our young people are interested in their church and its doctrinal principles.

The encampment has been operated successfully on the plan of finance recommended by the synod in 1928. Starting with a $28.00 deficit left over from the 1928 encampment, the first encampment held at Decatur in 1929 was brought to a close with all bills paid in full, and since that time the board has been enabled to report a small balance in the treasury at the close of each and every year.

The encampment work has had the effect of showing what can be done through consecrated, co-operative effort.

### RELATION TO THE CHURCH AT LARGE

Although remotely situated from the center of the denominational activities, Texas Cumberland Presbyterians have ever regarded themselves as vitally related to the church as a whole, in which there is no north, south, east, or west, sharing alike in the responsibilities and honors that have grown out of that relationship. We have benefited from and supported its institutions. Since 1932 we have had the privilege of having one of our denominational institutions, the orphans' home located in our midst, at Denton, Texas.

Texas has been host to the General Assembly eight times, its meeting places in Texas being as follows: Jefferson (1875), Austin (1881, Waco (1885), Dallas (1904), Corsicana (1908), Dallas (1918), Austin (1924), Olney (1930). This year (1936) the General

Assembly is convening in San Antonio, which will be the ninth General Assembly of the Cumberland Presbyterian Church to be held in Texas.

The first moderator of the General Assembly whom Texas furnished was Rev. T. B. Wilson, who was moderator of the General Assembly in 1859. Since that time, Texas has furnished the following moderators: Rev. A. Templeton (1880), Rev. E. B. Crisman (1886), Rev. J. M. Halsell (1900), Rev. S. M. Templeton (1902), Judge F. H. Prendergast (1909), Judge William Clark (1915), Rev. I. K. Floyd (1926), Rev. J. L. Elliott (1931), and Rev. A. C. DeForest (1934). Other men have occupied this high office who have had a part in building the church in Texas, but we have mentioned only those who were representing Texas presbyteries at the time of their election.

## OUR HERITAGE

Texas Cumberland Presbyterians have more than a hundred years of glorious history to inspire us to go forward. This church was one of the pioneers in the evangelization of this great empire of the Southwest. Sumner Bacon, if not the first Protestant minister who ever preached in Texas, may safely be counted the first to locate permanently in Texas. There is documentary evidence that he was here as early as 1830, and not until comparatively recent times has the attempt been made to wrest from him the distinction of being the pioneer Protestant preacher of Texas. The Cumberland Presbyterian Church, which had its beginning on the frontier, has been used of God to do a work of pioneering on many frontiers, not least glorious of which is that which Texas Cumberland Presbyterians claim as their heritage.

The work of pioneering is not yet over. As a denomination, we are still engaged in the task of rebuilding. Meanwhile, vast fields beckon unto us. A Cumberland Presbyterian minister in Texas, replying to a letter of inquiry from a minister in the East who was preaching for another denomination, said, "There is a great field for the Cumberland Presbyterian Church in Texas, and workers are needed. In fact, the need is a serious one. But the preacher who succeeds in our church in Texas must have the spirit of the pioneers. He must be willing to make many sacrifices and self-denials." This statement made a profound impression on the other minister, and he said, "Lord, if you need pioneers in Texas, let me be one"; and to Texas he came.

There is still the need for pioneers who will venture all for Christ; but the whole responsibility does not rest on the preachers. The membership of the church is no less called to make sacrifices and self-denials than is the ministry; for "how shall they preach except they be sent?"

May we never forget the foundations on which our church has risen, nor neglect the "whosoever will" evangel which we have cherished through the years. May we not waste our energies in grieving over our losses, or comparing our present numerical strength with our former glory. This we do not believe is honoring to the Lord with whom "there is no restraint to save by many or by few." Rather may the fact that God has preserved us a distinct and peculiar people and permitted us to witness the rebuilding of our cause in so many places constitute a challenge to us to be adequately prepared to face the opportunities that await us. Let us look to the future. The glory of achievement lies ahead of us, and in proportion as we consecrate ourselves to the mission for which we believe God brought our church into existence will our hopes for the future be realized.

www.ingramcontent.com/pod-product-compliance
Lightning Source LLC
Chambersburg PA
CBHW020853090426
42736CB00008B/353